The Land of Many Names

Towards a Christian Understanding of the Middle East Conflict

Steve Maltz

Authentic
LIFESTYLE

First published 2003 by Authentic Lifestyle.
Reprinted 2003

09 08 07 06 05 04 03 8 7 6 5 4 3 2

Authentic Lifestyle is a division of Authentic Media,
9 Holdom Avenue, Bletchley, Milton Keynes, Bucks,
MK1 1QR, UK.

Distributed in the USA by Gabriel Resources,
P.O. Box 1047, Waynesboro, GA 30830-2047, USA

British Library Cataloguing in Publication Data
A catalogue record for this book is available from the
British Library

1-86024-287-1

Cover design by David Lund
Printed in Great Britain by
Cox and Wyman Ltd., Reading, Berkshire

Acknowledgements

Of course, ultimate thanks go to the Lord, God of the Universe, for the breath of life, for the gift of new life and for pulling the strings. As for the supporting cast . . .

Lots of people to thank, for different reasons:

My wife Monica, for being my rock for 22 years while I flounder about. My Mum and Dad for their constant encouragement (creative and financial, respectively). My boys Phil, Simon and Jony for various welcome distractions during the creative process.

Andy, Derek, Frances, Joseph, Mike and Liz for their help in the editing process.

Tony, Siv, Brian, Raju, Malcolm, Kit and Julia for their overall encouragement.

Trevor, Margaret, Pollie, David W, Simon, Sheila, Mrs Carr, Carole, Gerard, Christine, Mr Hirst, Michael H, Thurston, Michael D, JW Embry, Gwen, Moira, Cherrie, Bernard, Roseanne, Andrew and David F for their confidence in me and this book and putting their money where their mouth is.

Contents

Preface

In May 2002, I helped to man a stand at the Christian Resources Exhibition in Esher, Surrey. Folk from 21 different ministries were exhibiting under the banner *Why Israel?* and seeking to open dialogue with other Christians, whatever their background or perspective. Interestingly, my overriding impression from those four days was that the only people willing to discuss the matter were those who shared the viewpoints of the exhibitors. The folk at the *Rediscovering Palestine* stand observed similar behaviour.

This spoke volumes to me of the vast rift between those who are generally for Israel in the current conflict and those who aren't. It was not dissimilar to the family who see the Christian evangelists at the front door and hide behind the sofa, hoping they haven't been spotted through the window. They think they know what the visitors are going to say, they've heard it all before and they're not willing to start a fresh argument on the subject. 'Why don't they leave us alone?' is the cry. Yet you and I know that hiding your head in the sand is not the best answer when truth, and in this case eternal salvation, is at stake. The trouble is that this family doesn't know it!

Tragically, we Christians can be ignorant of our own blind spot, our unwillingness to see the other point of view. One side would stress that Christians should pursue justice and righteousness and, as with apartheid in South Africa, should side with those whom they see as the oppressed and downtrodden, the Palestinians. Others, equally motivated by the Bible, would agree in principle, but would stress God's integrity and faithfulness in terms of Old Testament covenants in relation to the land as God's promise to the Jews. How can there be such a division between Christians on such a vital issue?

How many times have you been approached by someone and asked the question 'So what do you think about what's happening in the Middle East?' How frustrated have you been in your inability to string together a few coherent words, let alone a solid, robust argument to support your views? You are not alone. Hours of study and a PhD are the minimum requirements here for a full understanding of the intricacies and subtleties of a situation that doesn't even have a history people can agree on!

No issue has split the Christian world more than the Israel/Palestine conflict, yet there is no current issue as confusing. Millions of words have been written and spoken about it, but how much of it has truly sunk in, how much of it has made sense, how much of it has been untainted by personal opinion or editorial slant? Jews and Zionists will tell you one thing and Arabs and Arabists will tell you the opposite! Surely they can't both be right, surely there can only be one truth, one set of proven historical events that can unravel the whole mess? Unfortunately it isn't that straightforward. The situation is so complex, puzzling and emotionally charged that it is well-nigh impossible to get an objective viewpoint – it is exceedingly difficult to find historical sources with no axes to grind, commentators who could be accepted as truly impartial.

Even now you have probably got an idea of where I'm coming from and, if you haven't, I'll give you a little clue: I am an English Jew who discovered Jesus, my Messiah, some 16 years ago. This makes me biased, yes? No, because, for a Christian, the truth must always come first, despite the consequences. So the signature verse for this book is: '*God is spirit, and his worshippers must worship in spirit and in truth*' (John 4:24).

Nothing is more important than absolute honesty in our worship, in how we present ourselves to God, in all our thoughts and actions. Being true to the Spirit who indwells us is paramount, and a vital part of this is our quest for the truth in *all* situations.

I ask you not to judge me before you have read what I have to say. Instead, feel free to judge me by the fruits of what you do read. If you are left with a deeper understanding of the heart of God, a new commitment to prayer and a new, or refreshed, love for both Jewish and Palestinian people, then the fruit is good. My earnest desire is to understand God's truth about the situation in the Middle East and then to share it with others. There can only be one truth, one authentic script for the ongoing drama. The time is coming when we will all have to take a stand on this key issue and I hope that this book will provide a useful signpost for you.

With regard to the subject of this book, people tend to fall into three groups: those who believe that Israel has in some way a divine mandate; those who believe that Israel has no divine mandate in any way; and those who haven't got a clue about the matter because people in the other two groups seem equally persuasive. This book has been written for all groups, to clear away the cobwebs and to provide you with sufficient information for an informed opinion on the subject.

If, having read this book, you are still confused, and then I have failed. If, having read this book, you are not spiritually invigorated and challenged, I have also failed. This is a hot topic. God doesn't want you to be lukewarm; He wants people to be His witnesses, not just to other Christians but to the world out there that has absolutely no clue what is going on and has no Rock to hold on to. What better way to introduce people to this Rock than to show them exactly who is in charge of a world situation that, humanly speaking, has *no workable solution*?

Introduction

Let's be clear about this now. Israel is a little place, about the same size as Wales. Surrounded by thousands of miles of oil-rich desert, it is populated by a vast, seething melting pot of different colours, cultures and cuisines. It's the holiest place for great religions whose scriptures argue against having holy places! It has a geography of extremes: snow-capped mountains in the north, lush green orchards in the west, barren desert in the south and the lowest place on Earth in the east! It is possible to start a car journey needing an overcoat in Jerusalem and be sunbathing an hour later by the Dead Sea! Can Wales boast all of that? It's also the world's foremost political and religious hotspot, giving rise to more United Nations resolutions than all other nations put together! It's both hated and loved by more people than any other. It's the most fascinating, mysterious and intriguing place in the world.

It is also the most misunderstood and confusing place. Its history is a murky web of truth, half-truth and no-truth, depending on your perspective and allegiance. Its very name provokes dissent. To Jews it is Eretz Israel, the

Land of Israel. To most Arabs it is Palestine. To many Christians, confused by the whole issue, it is the simple fudge of the Holy Land.

The world has changed a great deal since the end of the Second World War. The Cold War came and went as Eastern Europe passed from repression to liberation. Two superpowers became one and Britain more or less lost her empire. The rest of Europe has voluntarily unified, by mutual consent rather than by Nazi domination. Populations moved eastwards, westwards, northwards, and southwards, driven by war or deprivation. No continent has been unaffected by this mass movement of people.

Yet in one slip of land, a mere green and gold scar in the deserts of Araby, time has frozen. People are still arguing and killing each other over events that happened more than 30, 40, 50 years ago. The year 1948 provokes contrasting emotions for the people of the land – to Jews it was liberation from 1,900 years of persecution, to Arabs it was the Nakba, the catastrophe.

This book deals with the origins of the current crisis in Israel. It has been written to help you in your understanding of what is a very thorny but vital topic for the Church today. Starting with the earliest Bible promises, it includes a history of the land from biblical times through to the modern day. Finally, there is a summing-up and a look to the future, with the Bible and its promises as our reference.

It is my belief that we Christians must look beyond day-to-day politics and realise that the conflict is a *spiritual* conflict. The sooner we begin to look at it through spiritual eyes, the sooner we will wake up to the realities of the battles being fought in heavenly realms. These are exciting times, frightening times.

Prologue

The best way to approach a subject as emotive as this is to put one's cards on the table right at the start, so that there can be no misunderstandings or suspicions. To be as frank as I can, this is an attempt at a response to books[1] that claim to represent 'different theological perspectives' but tend to lean towards just one particular perspective. In fact, of the 12 contributors to one such book, 11 are in basic agreement that the promises of God to Abraham concerning the 'Promised Land' have now been inherited by the Church and that the State of Israel is nothing more than a blip of modern history.

Do we, as Christians, go with the flow and play it safe? Do we follow the majority view just because this is taught in many Bible colleges and theological schools in the UK? The impression seems to be that a good dose of 'formal biblical and theological study' provided at these establishments will put you right on this issue and clear your mind of such nonsense as the restoration of Israel!

Does this mean that the majority of us who have not had the benefit of a formal Christian education do not have the tools to read the Bible correctly? Does this mean that only theologians are properly equipped to deal with such thorny issues as the identity of Israel and the Church? Does that mean that there's no point in consulting the Bible (particularly the Old Testament) on these matters, because we will probably get it wrong? Do we ordinary Christians not have a duty to examine the issues for ourselves? Also, how do these educational establishments arrive at their theological position? In other countries, notably the USA, the majority of schools would take a totally different perspective. Are we not all studying the same Bible?

These are good questions to ask because there is a lot at stake. Although these issues are not as vital as one's personal salvation, they are important for many reasons, not least concerning the faithfulness of God in His dealings with His people. Therefore it is essential that every Christian, whatever their educational background, should prayerfully seek the truth on such a key issue. There is no sitting on the fence here; there can only be one truth.

In August 2002 a group of evangelical Christians in the USA sent a letter to President Bush expressing their concern at what they saw as imbalance in American policy towards the Middle East conflict.[2] One statement they made is worthy of note: *'Significant numbers of American evangelicals reject the way some have distorted biblical passages as their rationale for uncritical support for every policy and action of the Israeli government instead of judging all actions – of both Israelis and Palestinians – on the basis of biblical standards of justice.'* When we get to the stage where Christians openly accuse others of 'distorting biblical passages', it is time for us to truly seek God's face and examine how there can be such a split in the Body of Christ.

The arena of conflict is the cauldron of confusion known as hermeneutics, which, for you and me, is concerned with how we should read and apply the Bible. The two key skirmishes are, firstly, how much of the Bible should be taken literally and, secondly, to what extent do we read the Old Testament in the light of the coming of Jesus in the New Testament. The trick is getting the balance right between these two factors and it is fair to say that the differences of opinion are caused by different emphases being given to each of them.

One barrier to the acceptance of a pro-Israel view in the UK is our natural conservatism, a fear of being sucked into what is viewed by some as the 'lunatic fringe'. Interpreting some key scriptures in a certain way is not necessarily going to turn you into a full-blown extreme dispensationalist or end-time fanatic, leafing through one of the hundreds of books on the subject for clues to the prophetic apocalyptic timetable. One must not be ruled by such fears and you should trust yourself with a certain degree of discernment. Don't throw the baby out with the bathwater. Be real. We should be secure enough in our views to defend them to anyone.

It is all a matter of personal integrity. Be yourself. Be blessed.

NOTES

1 Prime examples are *Whose Promised Land* by Colin Chapman and *The Land of Promise* by Johnston & Walker.
2 Institute for Global Engagement, *Letter to President Bush*, August 5, 2002. The full text can be found at http://www.globalengagement.org/issues/2002/08/letter.htm

Chapter 1

Canaan

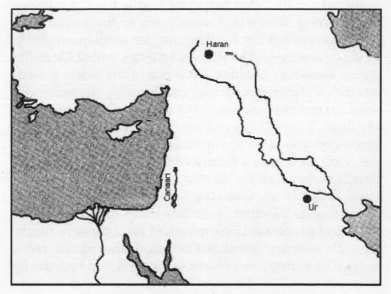

Fig. 1: **Abraham's journey to Canaan**

A good place to start would be the beginning, but the beginning of what? As we are focusing on the 'Land of many names', we'll start there, at a time in its history when it first became significant in the affairs of man.

Around 2000 BC the land was known as Canaan. It was the western end of a region that stretched from the Persian Gulf in the east to the Mediterranean in the west.

This region is known as the Fertile Crescent, because it is shaped like a crescent and consists of land that is well watered and easily cultivated. The inhabitants of Canaan at this time were known, believe it or not, as Canaanites, an agricultural people who shared a culture and religion with many of the other tribes and nations that surrounded them.

Little did they know at the time that about 800 miles eastwards, at the other tip of the Fertile Crescent, things were stirring, things that were going to have significant consequences not just for them but for mankind right up to the present day. The place was a city called Ur in the region known as Chaldea. Ur is one of the oldest recorded cities and its ruins are still visible today, though you'll need to travel to the edge of the al-Hajar Desert in Iraq to see them. It was also a cult centre for the worship of the moon god, called (rather appropriately) Sin.

Living there was a family of Chaldean idol-worshippers. The head of the family was Terah and his son's name was Abram. One day Terah was struck by wanderlust and, together with his son, daughter-in-law Sarai and grandson Lot, embarked on a massive northwesterly journey towards Canaan, hundreds of miles away. The journey must have exhausted him because he only got as far as Haran, and he died there at the ripe old age of 205.

The source of Terah's wanderlust was not some trivial whim but a serious prompting from God Himself and, after Terah's demise, the mantle falls on his son Abram to fulfil the divine calling.

We read of this calling in the 12th chapter of Genesis. In verse 1 God tells Abram to get moving again, to *'a land I will show you'*, and in the subsequent two verses we read the following:

'I will make you into a great nation and I will bless you; I will make your name great, and you will be a blessing. I will bless those who bless you, and whoever curses you I will curse; and all peoples on earth will be blessed through you.'

Two questions are posed here: Who exactly is this great nation, and how will all peoples on earth receive these promised blessings? To Abram it was quite simple: it was a promise from God that went beyond all logic and common sense. After all, how were he and his barren wife, both in their 70s, going to produce a 'great nation' if they hadn't even produced their first child yet? As for blessing 'all the peoples on earth', that must have made them chuckle!

This is where our troubles begin. It is fair to say that this promise, repeated and expanded in Genesis chapters 13, 15 and 17, is the root cause of the divisions within the Christian community that were mentioned in the Prologue. To be precise it is the *interpretation* of these verses that is causing the bother and so it is worth spending time strolling through the Bible text, to see what it is that has caused such conflict between Christians.

So first let's decide exactly how we are going to read these verses.

The obvious approach is the one that we take when we read anything, whether a shopping list or a weighty novel. It is what you are doing now. You read it word for word and your understanding is fed by exactly what you are reading. This is called the *literal* approach. If your shopping list tells you 'a bunch of bananas', you don't go and buy a loaf of bread! The literal approach to reading the Bible is defined as 'following the plain and obvious meaning of the text'. It was the approach taken by the earliest Christians and, significantly, by the Protestant reformers such as Luther and Calvin, as a response to the corruptions wrought by the Catholic Church, which had developed a system of reading the Bible – the *allegorical* approach – that allowed it to interpret scripture in a highly symbolic fashion. In some cases, this amounted to coaxing the Bible to say whatever they wanted!

Of course, this doesn't mean that everything in the Bible is easy to read and understand: we must bear in mind that it was written centuries ago in the language and cultural alphabet of the Hebrews of the time. As well as straightforward narrative, there is poetry and a lot of symbolism alien to our ears. But if we look for the plain meaning first and accept that a little more work on our part is needed in places to draw the meaning out, then we can't go far wrong. We read again the words of Genesis 12:

> *'I will make you into a great nation and I will bless you; I will*
> *make your name great, and you will be a blessing. I will bless*
> *those who bless you, and whoever curses you I will curse; and*
> *all peoples on earth will be blessed through you.'*

The plain meaning of this is that Abram himself is going to be a great nation, through whom everyone on earth will be blessed. Now one man does not constitute a nation, so simple logic tells us that this passage is talking about his descendants (borne out in verse 7). The obvious understanding is that this points to Jesus, a distant descendant, through whom the whole world will be blessed. This makes sense and all Christians would agree with this conclusion.

Back to our story. Abram was the first man to be called a Hebrew, a name coming from Eber, an ancestor and a descendant of Shem who, in turn, was a son of Noah. It is from the name Shem that we get the words 'Semite', a term usually used for anyone of Middle-Eastern origin, and 'anti-Semitic', curiously only used in relation to Jews. Shem, who spent all that time in the Ark with Noah and his family, was still living in Abram's lifetime. Mind you, he was 465 years old at the time of Abram's call from God and probably the oldest man alive. What conversations they could have had together! Even more interesting was the fact that Canaan, whose clans now filled this new land, was Shem's nephew and possibly also alive. What interesting reunions they could have had!

So God called Abram and, as a reward for dragging himself and his family hundreds of miles across the desert at the creaky old age of 75 years, He promised him that he would produce a great nation. God spoke to Abram again, pointed to the land around him and, despite the fact that it was inhabited at that time by the Canaanites, promised the land to his offspring in Genesis 12:7. In the next chapter – after Abram's brief sojourn in Egypt and a minor squabble with his nephew Lot – God repeated the promise, but added the words, in Genesis 13:15, '*All the land that you see I will give to you and your offspring for ever.*' Those two extra words '*for ever*' seem to make a big difference, as a time element is now brought in, adding a dimension of permanence to the deal. Just like the loving Father that He is, God coaxes Abram to stroll around the land: 'Yes, son, this will all be yours'. The rent book for the land of Canaan had been handed over in that one act 4,000 years ago.

For a clearer understanding, we move on to chapter 15 in the Genesis account and to a defining moment in the career of Abram. This is when God's promises to Abram became God's covenant with Abram.

This leads us to an important question. What is a covenant? It's not a word that we tend to use much these days, so it's important that we understand it. A covenant is a contract between two parties, a binding agreement. This covenant/contract came about when Abram, in a very human way, asked for assurances. After all, he was well past his prime and had produced no heir, yet here was God promising this land to his descendants! He needed a few more details, even though he never for once doubted that God would remain true to His promises. So God gave Abram the assurances he asked for.

'When the sun had set and darkness had fallen, a smoking brazier with a blazing torch appeared and passed between the pieces' (Genesis 15:17).

He made a covenant with Abram, in the custom and manner that such transactions were conducted in those days, except for one thing – only God signed the contract. Only God 'passed between the pieces', which meant that only God had to fulfil the covenant conditions – the covenant was going to be *unconditional*, as far as Abram and his descendants were concerned. There would be no conditions for Abram to fulfil – or break. This meant that God would *never* have reason to tear it up.

However much Abram's descendants tried – and boy, did they try in their chequered history – there were no actions, whether idolatry or faithlessness or whatever, that would cause this covenant to be torn up or nullified.

And what were the words of this unconditional covenant? You can read the words of the covenant in Genesis 15:18–21: *'On that day the Lord made a covenant with Abram and said, "to your descendants I give this land, from the river of Egypt to the great river, the Euphrates – the land of the Kenites, Kenizzites, Kadmonites, Hittites, Perizzites, Rephaites, Amorites, Canaanites, Girgashites and Jebusites. "'*

The plain *literal* reading of this verse is that Abram's descendants will inherit, by divine promise, the land indicated. There are no conditions, no time frame, so for now we won't add any of our own. All that is left is to decide what exact area is being referred to in this description. We're looking at an area stretching from Egypt in the west to modern day Iraq in the east and Syria (or arguably Turkey) in the north. One thing is certain about this – the land that God speaks of here has never at any time been seen, in its totality, as the 'Land of Israel', even at the time of King Solomon's empire, which, according to 2 Chronicles 9:26, stretched from *'the River (Euphrates) to the land of the Philistines, as far as the border of Egypt'* but certainly didn't stretch as far north as the lands of the Hittites. The full area promised by God to Abram's descendants has yet to be settled by any one people claiming this promise. Interesting.

At this point, it is worth bearing in mind that there are other interpretations of the verses examined so far. Objections have been raised to some of the assumptions made. These will be covered shortly, but in the meantime please indulge me as I build my case.

A literal reading of the biblical account seems quite clear and explicit. The land belongs, by divine decree, to the descendants of Abram. The only things that we need to get clear are:

1. Who are the descendants of Abram?
2. What are the conditions of this very generous offer?

To answer the first question we have to look at one of Abram's very human failings, his impatience. His wife Sarai talked him into sleeping with Hagar, her Egyptian maidservant, to 'hurry things along' and give God a hand – after all, Abram was now 85 years old and Sarai wasn't far behind him, age-wise.

Out of this union was born Ishmael, the 'father of the Arab nations'. Surely, you may say, the Arab people can claim that Abram, the father of Ishmael, was their ancestor too, and so the biblical promises concerning the land could be theirs as well as for the Jews?

In fact, God does give them specific promises. We read them in Genesis 16:10–12. Firstly, '*I will so increase your descendants that they will be too numerous to count*', and secondly, referring to Ishmael, '*He will be a wild donkey of a man; his hand will be against everyone and everyone's hand against him, and he will live in hostility towards all his brothers.*'

But as far as the covenant promises of the land are concerned, their claim is null and void according to the Word of God, which we will discover as the story unfolds.

God's relationship with Abram – now 99 years old – deepens in Genesis 17, when the covenant is confirmed and some small print added:

> '*The whole land of Canaan, where you are now an alien, I will give as an everlasting possession to you and your descendants after you; and I will be their God*' *(verse 8).*

Again, the land is mentioned – Canaan is confirmed as an *everlasting* possession for Abram and his descendants. God also confirms the everlasting nature of the covenant, reminding Abram of the sheer numbers of his descendants and declaring that He, the God of Abram, will also be the God of his descendants. Furthermore, Abram gets a name change: from now on he will be *Abraham*, meaning 'father of many nations', confirming God's earlier promise to make him into a great nation.

The next verse is where some may question the unconditional nature of the covenant. In verse 9, God says *'As for you, you must keep my covenant, you and your descendants after you . . .'* He seems to be laying down conditions for Abraham and his descendants, that they must keep the covenant, or else. Does this mean that the covenant *can* be broken and rendered null and void? The answer is given in the next verse.

> *'This is my covenant with you and your descendants after you, the covenant you are to keep: Every male among you shall be circumcised' (verse 10).*

This was the only condition that God imposed. If Abraham's descendants were to stop circumcising their children, then they would individually be cut off from the covenant. But the unconditional nature of the covenant between God and Abraham and his descendants regarding the land itself was 'as safe as houses'.

To return to our first question – who are the descendants of Abraham as far as the unconditional covenant is concerned – it's all explained in Genesis 17:15–22.

Firstly, Sarai's name is changed to *Sarah*. Then God blesses her, telling her that she will be the 'mother of nations'. He tells Abraham that he will produce a son, Isaac, with the 90-year-old Sarah and adds: *'I will establish my covenant with him as an everlasting covenant for his descendants after him'* (verse 19). It couldn't be clearer – Isaac inherits the blessings.

What about Ishmael, then? Well, God repeats what He said earlier about Ishmael's descendants being fruitful, but He also adds these words, in verse 21: *'but my covenant I will establish with Isaac . . . '* (my emphasis). Again, couldn't be clearer.

If we fast-forward historically and biblically to Genesis 25, we witness the death of Abraham at the grand old age of 175 and we also see his son Isaac become an old man. There's not much said about Isaac as an individual, apart from his partiality to eating choice young goats, but his son Jacob more than makes up for it. Jacob has a twin brother called Esau, but God makes it clear, as He did earlier with Isaac and Ishmael, that Jacob is the covenant child. It was Jacob who received his father's blessing in Genesis 27:27–29 and it was he who dreamed of the 'stairway to heaven' in Genesis 28:12–17, when God repeated the contents of the covenant He had made with his grandfather Abraham concerning the land – *'I will give you and your descendants the land on which you are lying'* (verse 13). Of course, it was Jacob who was renamed Israel after wrestling with God at Peniel and it was his sons who were to become the 'children of Israel', the Israelites, from whom the Jewish nation sprang forth, and who now, some 4,000 years later, are living proof of the covenant made with Abraham by God.

It's tempting now to declare 'that's that', but it's not that simple, I'm afraid. It is now time to backtrack and examine the objections to the approach I have taken. My approach has been to look at the text just as it has been written, taking the meaning from a plain reading of the text.

Others, though, would disagree with this approach. Firstly, there are some specific objections to how the text has been interpreted.

Some would say that despite what the literal reading seems to imply, there were conditions attached to this covenant with Abraham, and the descendants of Abraham could lose their rights to the land if they broke them. To be frank, you have to bend your logic considerably to get a grip on these conditions.

They wonder about what would have happened if Abram hadn't made the journey to Canaan (Genesis 12:1). Or what if his descendants didn't become a blessing to the nations (Genesis 12:2)? Or what if Abraham didn't 'walk before God' (Genesis 17:1)? Well, history tells us that he *had*, they *did* and he *did* and so any further discussion on this is pointless.

Others look at the promise of land given to Abraham, saying that surely this promise was fulfilled at the time of Joshua and so has no relevance to us today. This objection will be discussed in the next chapter.

The second and most common alternative perspective is to re-interpret the covenant with Abraham in the light of the fact that Jesus Christ has since come into the world. Because of this, they say, some key themes of the Old Testament must be re-evaluated. This is an important issue and must not be underestimated. But neither must it be overestimated.

The problem is trying to decide exactly *which* parts of the Old Testament are affected by the coming of the Messiah. This is where we get differences in opinion because we are naturally departing from the safe haven of an objective literal reading of the text and we are moving into the subjective areas of allegorising or spiritualising the text. In other words, because we accept that Jesus changes everything, we have to accept that, for some people, certain Bible texts now attract new meanings determined by some scholars' understanding of how the Old Testament must be read in the light of the New Testament. We have the benefit of history to show us the results of such teachings, first expounded by some of the Church Fathers in the early years of Christianity, teachings heavily influenced by the Greek culture of the time.

The 'uneducated' reader of the Old Testament is now told that s/he would be mistaken in reading parts of it as straight narrative, because we may not be getting the full story. But who sets the rules? Most of us simply don't have the training to be able to understand the theological complexities of this approach.

In some places we have little difficulty, for instance when we identify Jesus as the fulfilment of so many Old Testament promises and prophecies, including the one in Genesis 12:3 that we read earlier. We read such verses and even sing them, at Christmas time. This makes sense as these show the Old Testament pointing to the New Testament. But to have to read the Old Testament with one eye on the text and the other on a whole library of concordances and commentaries is beyond many ordinary Christians. They simply don't have the time. Surely reading the Bible was not meant to be *this* difficult?

So let us again read the original wording of the covenant with Abraham (when he was just plain Abram).

> 'I will make you into a great nation and I will bless you; I will make your name great, and you will be a blessing. I will bless those who bless you, and whoever curses you I will curse; and all peoples on earth will be blessed through you' (Genesis 12:2–4).

> 'The whole land of Canaan, where you are now an alien, I will give as an everlasting possession to you and your descendants after you; and I will be their God' (Genesis 17:8).

Now, as already mentioned, not all Christians would read these scriptures in the same way. In fact, Christians tend to fall into one of two camps.

The first would take the plain meaning of the text, reading it *literally*, and take these promises to mean that there is a role for Abraham's descendants, the Jewish people – and the land of Israel – in the Christian age.

The second read the text *symbolically* and say that there is absolutely no role at all for the Jewish people or the land of Israel in the Christian age.

The first group tend to stress the continuity between the Old and New Testaments, whereas the second group tend to elevate the New over the Old, saying that all things changed with the advent of Jesus the Messiah.

For the purpose of this book, I will give names to these groups based on the imagery of Romans 11:17, *'If some of the branches have been broken off, and you, though a wild olive shoot, have been grafted in among the others and now share in the nourishing sap from the olive root . . .'*

The first group, the literal readers of scripture, I shall call *Mr Roots*, to identify them with the oldest part of the olive tree, and the second group, the scripture spiritualisers, I shall call *Mr Shoots*, identifying them with the newest parts of the olive tree.

Mr Roots would look at the plain meaning of these verses, which tell him that the descendants of Abraham – the Jews – are to become a great nation, living in a land promised to them by God as a permanent habitation and out of whom there would come great blessings to the world, through Jesus.

Mr Shoots would agree with the bit about Jesus being the one through whom all peoples on earth will be blessed, as he has no doubt that Jesus was a physical descendant of Abraham. But he *wouldn't* agree with most of the other stuff.

Firstly, Mr Shoots and his friends disagree about who exactly is the 'great nation'. Some appeal to the Book of Revelation, quoting from Revelation 7:4, the '*144,000 from all the tribes of Israel*', though not explaining who exactly is being referred to. Others are more specific, regarding all believers, Jew and Gentile, as this 'great nation'.

There is even more confusion among the Mr Shoots group about what is the 'promised land'. One popular scripture is Matthew 5:5, where they re-interpret 'Blessed are the meek, for they will inherit the earth' as 'Blessed are the meek, for they will inherit the *land*', remarking that the qualification for inheriting the physical 'promised land' is meekness – a quality, they would say, that is displayed more by Christians than Jews. So in their view the land belongs to Christians. Others spiritualise the whole thing, saying that the 'promised land' refers to heaven, or the Body of Christ, or the kingdom of God. Mathew Henry talks of a 'heavenly Canaan' promised, again, to the *spiritual* descendants.[1]

When answering the question 'Whose God will He be', Mr Shoots looks forward to Revelation 7:9 to the '*great multitude . . . standing before the throne*'. The general consensus has God transferring His attention and love from Jews to the *spiritual* descendants, the Christians. Jews would now be no more loved or cared for than any other nation on earth.

Now these are all clever people, with a multitude of theological qualifications and decades of Christian service between them. But that doesn't make them infallible. Paul tells us in 1 Corinthians 27:1 '*But God chose the foolish things of the world to shame the wise . . .*' We mustn't be fazed by cleverness because, after all, most of the brightest brains of our age are still dead in their sins (i.e. they are non-Christians). Equally, we mustn't neglect our brain cells out of laziness or neglect. Balance is what we need: head and heart, word and spirit.

Was there anything the Jews could do to nullify or ruin this covenant? The answer seems to be *no*. We are told that the covenant was and still is unconditional and everlasting. But what is clear is that God holds the title deeds to the land and the Jews are the only tenants in the contract: *'because the land is mine and you are but aliens and my tenants'* (Leviticus 25:23).

In the next chapter, we will examine how these new tenants found themselves in their new home.

NOTES

1 Mathew Henry, *Complete Commentary on the Whole Bible*, Genesis 15.

Chapter 2

The Land of Milk and Honey

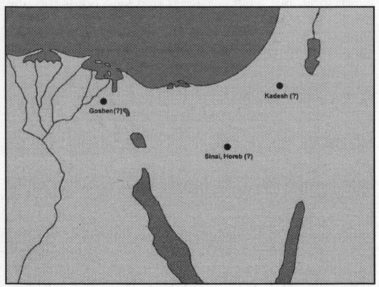

Fig. 2: **Conquering the 'Land of Milk and Honey'**

The promises given by God to Abraham must have seemed a bit far-fetched as his descendants, the Israelites, sweated in the Egyptian quarries and building sites of Pharaoh. After all, hadn't the Lord promised the land *'from the river of Egypt to the great river, the Euphrates'* (Genesis 15:18–21)? It must have seemed a sick joke to those Hebrew slaves, for whom the 'river of Egypt' was a place where they drew their sustenance between work shifts. How on earth had they got into that predicament?

God did warn them, after all. He did tell Abraham that his descendants were going to spend a good 400 years or so as 'strangers in a strange land' and Egypt was never one of Abraham 's favourite places, no doubt a reminder of his woman troubles. First, there was that delicate matter between Pharaoh and Sarah ('She's my sister – no, sorry, she's my wife!'). Then, of course, there was the matter of frisky Hagar the Egyptian, the mother of Ishmael, but God's plans are His own and it was necessary for Abraham's descendants, led by his great-grandson, Joseph, to settle in Egypt 'until the sin of the Amorites reached its full measure' (Genesis 15:16). So they arrived in Egypt as proud guests of 'our brother the governor' and watched as things went steadily downhill, ending up as slaves to a new Pharaoh many years later.

Then Moses came along, and on that first Passover night, the first small step was made towards fulfilling God's promise when around two million Israelites made a beeline eastwards for the Red Sea and freedom. They were coming home, to the land promised by God to Abraham all those years earlier, but it wasn't going to be that easy as they spent 40 years circling around the Sinai desert getting nowhere. It was their own fault because it didn't have to be that way.

The first year had been spent receiving the Law at Horeb (Sinai). It was there that Moses received the Ten Commandments (and the other 603 rules and regulations recorded in the Books of Moses – primarily Leviticus and Deuteronomy). These constituted what has become known as the Mosaic covenant or 'the Laws of Moses'.

Ah, a covenant. Does this take the place of the old covenant with Abraham? No, certainly not, because, if you remember, the Abrahamic covenant was unconditional.

'The whole land of Canaan, where you are now an alien, I will give as an everlasting possession to you and your descendants after you; and I will be their God' (Genesis 17:8).

This new covenant with Moses contained a whole list of rules and regulations, some major, some minor, all perfectly breakable.

'When Moses went and told the people all the Lord's words and laws, they responded with one voice, "Everything the Lord has said we will do"' (Exodus 24:3).

Yeh, right!

This covenant, the Mosaic covenant, was a conditional covenant, meaning that it could be broken. Deuteronomy 28 contains a list of blessings and curses attached to this covenant: blessings if the people followed God's commands and curses if they didn't. As we shall see later, subsequent Jewish history to the present day represents the outworking of this covenant.

The second year in the desert was spent travelling to Kadesh, where it all went horribly wrong. You can read about it in Numbers 13 and 14. It seemed that God's promises of the land were about to be realised. The Israelites were poised at the edge of Canaan; the land was theirs for the taking. All they needed was sufficient faith in the God who had delivered them from Egypt and sustained them with miracle after miracle.

They were at the edge of the land of Canaan and they halted. Twelve men were sent to spy out the land. Their names and lineage were proudly recorded in Numbers 13:4–15. Ten of them came back with tall tales of giants and demonic offspring and every excuse not to progress further – 'Hey, chaps, it's been fun but perhaps it's time we went home – to Egypt'. These men's names were never again to appear in the Bible, whereas the only two to have a positive report of the land – Joshua and Caleb – became heroes of the faith.

Because the Israelites chose to believe the ten doom-merchants, this incredible lack of faith doomed the entire adult generation (except for Joshua and Caleb) to wander around in circles for up to 38 years and never to enter the 'Land of Milk and Honey'.

So, had their lack of faith in God, their deliverer from Egypt, nullified God's covenant with Abraham? Moses has more to say on this subject as we now find him, at Moab, near the end of his life, a tired old man of 120 years.

First, let us consider the situation. We look at the covenant that God made with Moses at Horeb (the Ten Commandments and all that) and ask ourselves 'Does this replace the one that God made with Abraham about 600 years earlier?' This is a key question because, if the answer is yes, as some people proclaim, there are two major consequences:

1. God breaks promises. After telling Abraham that His promises to him are everlasting, despite any-thing Abraham or his descendants might do to pro-voke Him, He's now adding conditions! Think about it. Christians are saved through the 'New Covenant' that basically sets out the rules and con-ditions by which we can attain salvation. Suppose God just turned round and said 'Hold on, it hasn't

exactly gone according to plan. I'm changing my mind and adding one or two new conditions. Sorry.' We'd be very worried people, wouldn't we?

2. Which parts of God's covenant with Abraham now have conditions slapped on them? The promises of spiritual blessings? Becoming a great nation? Inheriting the land? It all gets very fuzzy.

If we look at Deuteronomy 29:1, we see what Moses has to say:

'These are the terms of the covenant the Lord commanded Moses to make with the Israelites in Moab, in addition to the covenant he had made with them at Horeb' (my emphasis).

I hear the cry, 'Oh no, not *another* covenant'! The answer is yes and no. I hear a new cry: 'Oh no, not *another* ambiguous statement. What's all this yes and no business?'

It does say that at Moab God makes a new covenant in *addition* to the one He made a generation earlier with Moses at Horeb. So there is another covenant, called by some the *Palestinian* covenant (unfortunate name really), but is it a *new* covenant?

The full text is in Deuteronomy 29 and 30. What we see here is an explanation of how God can show both His *faithfulness*, by upholding His promises given to Abraham, and His *righteousness*, by rewarding or punishing His people according to their behaviour. Basically, the 'Palestinian covenant' allows the Abrahamic and the Mosaic covenants to sit side by side, with no conflict of interest.

What it first shows, in Deuteronomy 29, is the consequences of sin. This is the *conditional* bit, the stuff from the Mosaic covenant. This tells God's people that, despite all the good things God did for His people in the wilderness and in battle, the consequence of their worshipping the false gods of the Canaanites is going to be a curse on the land and exile from it.

This is not the whole story because no exile from the land could ever be permanent: the Abrahamic covenant saw to that. So we read in Deuteronomy 30:2–10 that despite the exile from the land, a day will come when the Abrahamic covenant will kick in and the exiles will return to the land: *'Even if you have been banished to the most distant land under the heavens, from there the Lord your God will gather you and bring you back'* (verse 4).

What this 'new' covenant at Moab, this Palestinian covenant, does is to warn the Israelites that the punishment for unfaithfulness and disobedience will be exile from the 'Land of Milk and Honey', but the right to the land will never be taken from them and one day in the future it will be theirs again. Their lease will never be torn up, even if the landlord may kick them out temporarily for rule breaking!

Further light is shed on this in the New Testament, in Galatians 3:17: *'What I mean is this: The law, introduced 430 years later, does not set aside the covenant previously established by God and thus do away with the promise.'* This further emphasises the difference between the covenants made with Abraham and Moses.

Mr Shoots would quote from a number of verses here to say that the promises of the land were conditional on their behaviour:

Leviticus 18:24–25: *'Do not defile yourselves in any of these ways, because this is how the nations that I am going to drive out before you became defiled. Even the land was defiled; so I*

> *punished it for its sin, and the land vomited out its inhabi-*
> *tants.'*

> Leviticus 26:32–35: *'I will lay waste the land, so that your*
> *enemies who live there will be appalled. I will scatter you*
> *among the nations and will draw out my sword and pursue*
> *you. Your land will be laid waste, and your cities will lie in*
> *ruins. Then the land will enjoy its sabbath years all the time*
> *that it lies desolate and you are in the country of your enemies;*
> *then the land will rest and enjoy its sabbaths. All the time that*
> *it lies desolate, the land will have the rest it did not have dur-*
> *ing the sabbaths you lived in it.'*

Yet, if he were to read on in this chapter, to verses 40–45,
he would find this:

> *'But if they will confess their sins and the sins of their fathers –*
> *their treachery against me and their hostility towards me, which*
> *made me hostile towards them so that I sent them into the land of*
> *their enemies – then when their uncircumcised hearts are hum-*
> *bled and they pay for their sin, I will remember my covenant with*
> *Jacob and my covenant with Isaac and my covenant with*
> *Abraham, and I will remember the land. For the land will be*
> *deserted by them and will enjoy its sabbaths while it lies desolate*
> *without them. They will pay for their sins because they rejected*
> *my laws and abhorred my decrees. Yet in spite of this, when they*
> *are in the land of their enemies, I will not reject them or abhor*
> *them so as to destroy them completely, breaking my covenant*
> *with them. I am the Lord their God. But for their sake I will*
> *remember the covenant with their ancestors whom I brought out*
> *of Egypt in the sight of the nations to be their God. I am the Lord.'*

Mr Shoots is willing to proclaim the curses for Jewish
disobedience, but is strangely unwilling to read on and

accept that God always provides the possibility of blessings for obedience, through the promises of the covenant with Abraham. His thinking is that because of God's rejection of the Jewish people, He is unwilling to implement the verses after verse 39 of Leviticus 26. 'How can God bless a people He has already cursed?' is his thinking, putting restrictions on God's behaviour in the process.

It's the attitude of the 'stay-at-home' son in the story of the Prodigal (Luke 15:11–32). One son blows his inheritance on wild living and returns to his father in

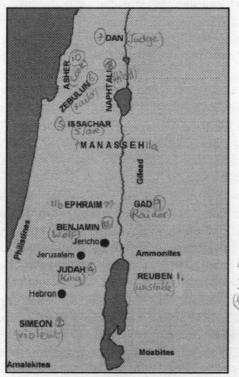

Fig 3: **Allocation of the Tribes**

repentance, but the other one is unwilling to accept the possibility of restitution and is consumed with 'righteous anger'. So it is with Mr Shoots, unwilling to believe that, contrary to the very essence of Christian teaching concerning repentance and restitution, God refuses to grant second chances to the Jewish people.

The position held by Mr Shoots can in some situations, as we shall see later, force him into a cavalier approach to reading scripture, to the extent that whole passages of scripture must be ignored, in order not to 'upset the apple cart'.

Returning to our story we find that it was the children of Moses' doomed generation who eventually entered the land of Canaan, led by Joshua. About 600 years after the time of Abraham, the Promised Land now started to become a reality. Numbers 34 records that before Moses died he drew up a map of the land to be conquered. This land was to be divided up and allocated to nine and a half of the tribes of the Israelites – the other two and a half tribes had already been allotted land on the east side of the River Jordan. He then coaxed his surprisingly strong 120-year-old bones up Mount Nebo, where he died in full sight of the Land of Milk and Honey, with God's final words reminding him of His oath concerning this land.

So who was really living in the land at that time? Amorites, Midianites, Perizzites, Jebusites and Hivites, collectively known as Canaanites. The sin of the Amorites had reached its full measure (Genesis 15:16) and the Israelites were on their way to put things right. What the children of Israel did to the Canaanites, as instructed by the Lord God, would have seriously upset many modern Christian liberals. Nothing short of complete annihilation was on the cards here. 'How could God be so brutal?' is their cry. What could these people have done to reap such judgement?

We read about the ways of the Canaanites in Leviticus 18. Here we find a whole list of forbidden relationships and unnatural sexual practices – most of which are currently in vogue in today's decadent society – and which were subjects of God's wrath.

God's instructions are given in Deuteronomy 20:16–18: *'However, in the cities of the nations the Lord your God is giving you as an inheritance, do not leave alive anything that breathes. Completely destroy them – the Hittites, Amorites, Canaanites, Perizzites, Hivites and Jebusites – as the Lord your God has commanded you. Otherwise, they will teach you to follow all the detestable things they do in worshipping their gods, and you will sin against the Lord your God.'*

This episode has upset many Christians, who find it hard to reconcile this (they say) 'vengeful' God with the loving God of the New Testament. Some of them use it as another bludgeon against the Old Testament as an 'inferior' revelation of God. Others seek to diminish it in other ways. Some, seeing Jesus' coming as a cause for the re-interpretation of much of the Old Testament, say that Jesus would never have acted in the brutal ways that Joshua did, for the same reason that Joshua could never have understood the love of God as expressed in the life, death and resurrection of Jesus. The reason, they say, is that God only acts according to the culture and understanding of the day.

This may seem neat and tidy, but does it mean that nowadays God has to remember to calm down in case He upsets Christians? According to them, the striking down of Ananias and Sapphira in Acts 5 must have been an embarrassing mistake, to say nothing of the promises in store for our sinful world in the judgements promised by Jesus in Matthew 24. And how could David, the 'primitive' Old Testament king and psalmist, have understood ideas of death and resurrection when he wrote the Psalms? Remind yourself, whenever you hear a news report of some natural disaster or outrage that is 'of biblical proportions', that this present age is just as brutal and ignorant as the time of Joshua, and the presence of the Christian message in the world makes not an iota of difference to the ignorant men and women who perpetrate deeds every bit as evil and debauched as those of the ancient Canaanites. God is the same yesterday, today and forever. So is human nature.

Canaan was conquered in three campaigns and the land divided among the tribes of Israel (Joshua 13–21), in accordance with God's plans as given to Moses just before his death (see Figure 3). In modern-day terms, we are looking at the geographical area of Israel, Jordan and Lebanon.

Mr Shoots would quote from Joshua 11:23: '*So Joshua took the entire land, just as the Lord had directed Moses, and he gave it as an inheritance to Israel according to their tribal divisions. Then the land had rest from war.*' He would use this as fuel for his argument against the literal reading of the covenant with Abraham by saying that here we see the fulfilment of the land promises – after all, doesn't it say 'Joshua took the *entire* land'? 'Yes,' says Mr Roots, 'it does. But it says nothing about the land promised to Abraham, only that promised to Moses, a much smaller area.'

The land was conquered, but despite God's stern warnings and apparently brutal fulfilments it was not completely cleansed of idolatry and evil practices. As we enter the period of the judges, we find many remnants of the ancient peoples still very much alive and kicking. The Philistines occupied the southern coastal plains and Moab held the land to the east of the Dead Sea, with Edom to the south. Canaanites were still everywhere and the greatest sin of the Israelites was their failure to follow God's command to eliminate them. As a consequence, immoral practices filtered into the Israelite community. It didn't take long. It happened as soon as Joshua's generation passed away.

> *'Then the Israelites did evil in the eyes of the Lord and served the Baals. They forsook the Lord, the God of their fathers, who had brought them out of Egypt. They followed and worshipped various gods of the peoples around them. They provoked the Lord to anger because they forsook him and served Baal and the Ashtoreths' (Judges 2:11–13).*

Before we start tut-tutting, stop and think for a moment how far we in the UK have come since the end of the Second World War, from being a church-going country to becoming one that worships at the altar of pagan gods, ranging from celebrity worship to Tibetan worship in cathedrals. In the time it took the Israelites to forget their victories under Joshua (with God's provision), we have proudly moved into a self-proclaimed 'post-Christian' era, where God's values are undermined and His provisions taken for granted.

This period of the judges can be summarised in one circular sentence: When Israel listened to God all was well, but when they fell away they were shown the consequences of their sin (usually through experiences of war), which prompted them to cry out to God, who sent them a judge, who led them back to listening to Him.

Repeat this about 12 times – through such judges as Deborah, Gideon, Samson etc. – and you get the idea. Keep going in this vein for 350 years. You'd think they'd get the point after half a dozen times or so, but human nature says otherwise – how soon we forget what God has done for us and move on under our own steam, making the same mistakes again and again.

The Israelites were meant to be a holy nation, a nation under God, a theocracy. They were chosen to be a nation *apart*, living among the other nations, but apart from them. This was why it was for their own good to destroy the corrupt nations around them: not to satisfy the apparent bloodlust of the Deity but to keep God's people as pure and uncorrupted as possible. However, it was never going to be easy.

The Israelites were chosen not because they had an especially holy and righteous nature that was going to make it easy for them to fulfil their destiny. They were chosen because . . . they were chosen. *Someone* had to be chosen. It just happened to be them. If God had chosen Nigel the Barbarian instead of Abraham to leave his mud hut and trek over to Canaan and if Nigel had proved as willing as Abraham to fulfil his calling, then it could have been the Nigelites that found themselves in this Land of Milk and Honey. The point is that God could have chosen anyone and perhaps would have chosen Nigel if Abraham hadn't been so faithful, but Abraham passed the test and it was *his* descendants that found themselves burdened with this 'chosenness'.

Some, of course, had lived up to this honour, great men of faith like Jacob, Joseph, Moses and Joshua, but they were the exceptions. Once the Israelites had been established in the land for a few years, they started to cast jealous eyes around the other nations and yearned to be like them. In the west of the country, a new problem had presented itself – the Philistines. These were a seafaring and aggressive people, sailing in from the Mediterranean, who quickly established themselves along the coastal plain and then turned their beady eyes eastwards, towards the land settled by the Israelites. They had two great military advantages over the Israelites – they had chariots and they had iron – but they didn't have the missing ingredient, the *Lord God of the Universe*, as the famous episode with Samson and Delilah was to show. Nevertheless, the Israelites had grown complacent and soon began to forget that if God was on your side, no-one could come against you.

Instead, they began to look at the nations around them. These people had kings, who led them into battle, ruled them, made decisions for them. We want a king too! This was the cry of Israel in 1 Samuel 8 and they got the one they deserved, Saul. God had warned them, but did they listen? He told them that this king was going to take away their sons to fight dangerous wars and their daughters to be cooks and bakers, and would also take a proportion of their land, crops, slaves and flocks for his own use. No, we want a king! 'Then don't come running back to me when it all goes wrong!' adds God, in 1 Samuel 8:18. 'We don't care – give us a king, already!'

This first king of Israel was volatile, insecure and paranoid, which was probably God's punishment on Israel for showing such a lack of faith in Him and demanding a king in the first place. There were controls in place, in the person of the prophet Samuel, who was the mouthpiece of God during this time, but Saul wasn't always to listen – except, tragically, through a witch after Samuel's death – and this was to provide the seeds of his downfall. Saul eventually committed suicide in battle and left the kingdom of Israel in a worse shape than when he found it, largely due to the presence of the pesky Philistines in the west.

Saul was succeeded by King David, a man somewhat flawed but with a deep and practical faith in God. On the one hand he was an adulterer, a murderer and quite cruel in the manner of his retributions to those who crossed him, but on the other hand he was brave, a good military commander and administrator, a poet of genius (as the Psalms show) and, above all, a man aware of his sins and willing to deal with them before God. He was to roundly defeat the Philistines, the Moabites, the Edomites and the Ammonites and captured a whole swathe of Canaanite cities, as well as Jerusalem, which was to become his capital.

Jerusalem was captured around 1000 BC from the Jebusites, who were big-headed enough to taunt the Israelites standing outside the walls of the city, saying that even the blind and lame would be able to keep David out. While they posed along the heavily fortified walls, David's army were clambering through the water shaft, from where they entered the city and conquered it. Jews have had a continuous presence in this city ever since (albeit only just so at the time of the city's destruction by the Romans, but more of that later).

Ah, Jerusalem! At last, it appears in the pages of our story. No other city in history has attracted so much controversy. At the time of David, the Israelite nation had been divided into two main regions, Israel and Judah. Judah covered the south of the land, comprising not just the land allocated to the tribe of Judah but also that given to Simeon and Benjamin. The region of Israel consisted of the central and northern parts, covering the land given to Ephraim, Dan, Manasseh, Issachar, Zebulun, Naphtali and Asher. And Jerusalem was right on the boundary between the two, accessible to both regions.

'There are ten portions of beauty in the world. Nine are in Jerusalem, one in the rest of the world. There are ten portions

of suffering in the world. Nine in Jerusalem and one in the rest of the world.'

This quote from the *Avot de Rabbi Natan*, an ancient collection of rabbinic commentary, serves to highlight the importance of Jerusalem in world history – and it all really started with King David, who took the significant decision to make Jerusalem his capital city.

The matter of Jerusalem has been a key focus of the battles between Mr Roots and Mr Shoots. Mr Roots would point out that Jerusalem is mentioned 669 times in the Old Testament, not just in a historical sense (describing key points in its history) but also in a *prophetic* sense. Zechariah 12:2–3 records the Word of the Lord: *'I am going to make Jerusalem a cup that sends all the surrounding peoples reeling. Judah will be besieged as well as Jerusalem. On that day, when all the nations of the earth are gathered against her, I will make Jerusalem an immovable rock for all the nations. All who try to move it will injure themselves.'*

Yet Mr Shoots would seek to pooh-pooh any suggestion that Jerusalem has any current significance for the Jewish people, even going as far as to suggest that whenever we see Jerusalem mentioned, it is *Jesus* that is meant!

Needless to say, Jerusalem has been one of the key points of conflict between Judaism, Gentile Christianity and Islam, and we will be discussing this in detail a little later.

Back to King David, now ruling the 'United Kingdom' of Judah and Israel from Jerusalem, his new capital city. For all his positive virtues, it was David's shortcomings that defined history with regard to the 'Promised Land'. Because of his adultery with Bathsheba, God was to tell him, in 2 Samuel 12:10, '*The sword shall never depart from your house*', which set the scene for a lot of deep bother for the future 'House of David'.

These prophetic words found fulfilment with his very own son, the handsome Absalom, who tried to usurp his father's position as king. He was so bigheaded that he had a monument in his own honour erected near Jerusalem. Unfortunately, his big head contributed to his demise – literally. He got it stuck in an oak tree and ended up with three javelins in his heart, courtesy of the commander of David's army. (Joab)

The next king of Judah and Israel was Solomon, another son but David's chosen successor. Here was a man who started off so promisingly, with a once-only offer from God in a dream of whatever he wanted. He chose wisely: *wisdom* rather than a long life, riches or power. God was so pleased with this unselfish choice that He gave him the lot anyway, so Solomon had everything he could have needed and his reign was indeed very fruitful.

The nation prospered as never before; Solomon built a palace and the magnificent First Temple in Jerusalem and expanded the kingdom, his influence reaching as far as the river Euphrates to the north and Egypt to the west. He wrote poetry (Song of Songs), philosophy (Ecclesiastes) and wisdom (Proverbs). Was there anything he couldn't do? Well there was one thing – he had difficulty in restraining himself with the fairer sex. Seven hundred wives and three hundred concubines seemed to be overdoing it a bit, but it was in the *spiritual* rather than the physical realm that we see the dire consequences of these dalliances.

The clue is in 1 Kings 11:1–2, where it is noted that Solomon's lovers included those from nations with which God had forbidden His people to intermarry. The reason was to do with spiritual pollution and we see the consequences in verse 4: *'As Solomon grew old, his wives turned his heart after other gods, and his heart was not fully devoted to the Lord his God, as the heart of David his father had been.'* Verse 6 says, similarly, *'He did not follow the Lord completely, as David his father had done.'*

God reminds Solomon that, through his actions, he has *not kept the covenant*. This is serious stuff. What covenant was He referring to? This was easy, as it was clearly a reference to the first two of the Ten Commandments. Solomon had taken to other gods and had indulged in idol worship, acts prohibited under the covenant made with Moses (see Exodus 20:1–4). He had broken some of the terms of the covenant and, as he was King of Israel, the consequences would be dire indeed.

They were. God now vows that the kingdom will be taken from Solomon's family and given to one of his subordinates. This was going to happen in the next generation. Solomon was offered this mercy not because he deserved it, but for the sake of his father David. Also, as a measure of the esteem the Lord had for David, it was decreed that one tribe, Judah, was to remain, *'for the sake of David my servant and for the sake of Jerusalem which I have chosen'* (verse 13), *'the city where I chose to put my Name'* (1 Kings 11:36).

So, because of the sin of one man, Solomon, the united kingdom was going to be split in two, resulting in two separate people with two separate destinies.

Chapter 3

Israel and Judah

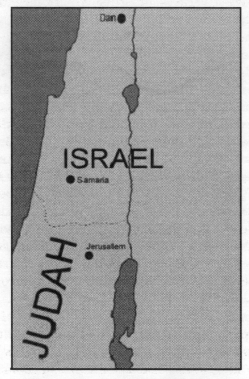

Fig. 4: **The Divided Kingdom**

What God had ordained came about, and this is how it happened.

Jeroboam was one of Solomon's favoured officials. He was told by the prophet Ahijah (1 Kings 11) that he would be God's instrument carrying out His judgements on Solomon, who by now was not particularly popular with his subjects. God even tempted Jeroboam with the promise that He would build a dynasty on him, equal to the one promised to David. The Lord undoubtedly had a smile on His face at the time because the conditions were the very same issue of 'keeping my statutes and commands' that was the foundation of the covenant with Moses. God knows the heart of man, and though He was gracious enough to offer this generous deal to Jeroboam, He knew that like everyone else born of mortal man, Jeroboam would slip up when it came to keeping his side of the bargain. That was the whole point of the covenant with Moses – sinful man was (and still is) incapable of fulfilling the conditions and will always fall short. It's just as well that a better covenant, the New Covenant, with different conditions, was to come along later!

On Solomon's death, his son Rehoboam succeeded him. He knew that because of Solomon's unpopularity towards the end of his reign, rebellion was in the air, so he took advice. Unfortunately, rather than listening to the wise elders, he took his advice from the young men he'd grown up with.

It was bad advice, resulting in a rebellion by Israel, the northern part of the kingdom. In accordance with God's pronouncement, Israel broke away from the 'United Kingdom' and, in fulfilment of Ahijah's prophecy, made Jeroboam their king. Their parting words to Rehoboam are given in 1 Kings 12:16: *'What share do we have in David, what part in Jesse's son? To your tents, O Israel! Look after your own house, O David!'*

Rehoboam was peeved. He summoned 180,000 fighting men to make war against the breakaway state of Israel. A bad idea; he had to be reminded by Shemaiah the prophet that this whole thing was the Lord's doing, so a civil war would not be his best move. He was left to take stock of the situation. All that remained for King Rehoboam was the house of Judah (including the smaller tribe of Benjamin) in the south, with Jerusalem as the capital, but if he only knew what was going to happen 'up north' he would have been counting his blessings!

It wasn't long before Jeroboam too broke God's covenant, ruining any chance he had to found a dynasty with God's blessings. As a result, the kingdom of Israel went from bad to worse. Jeroboam set the trend by making two golden calves and setting them up as gods in Bethel and Dan, saying *'Here are your gods, O Israel, who brought you up out of Egypt'* (1 Kings 12:28). He did this in order to stop the citizens of Israel making pilgrimages to the temple in Jerusalem, which was now in 'enemy' territory. He went on to build further pagan shrines and to ordain dodgy priests, piling sin upon sin and battering away at the Second Commandment until God could stay silent no longer. It was not surprising that Ahijah, the very same prophet who had set him up as king, should prophesy again with these words, in 1 Kings 14:9–10: *'You have done more evil than all who lived before you . . . I am going to bring disaster on the house of Jeroboam.'* There are hints concerning the nature of this punishment in verse 15: *'He will uproot Israel from this good land that he gave to their forefathers and scatter them beyond the River . . .'*

This prophecy was put on hold while subsequent rulers of Israel went from bad to worse, digging themselves further and further into the mire, with sordid tales of murder, massacre, idolatry and general mayhem.

Nadab succeeded Jeroboam and carried on in his father's evil ways for a few months until he and every last member of the doomed family dynasty were slaughtered by Baasha, who was to grab the throne of Israel for himself. Baasha continued in the same evil traditions, lasting for 24 years and, like Jeroboam, incurring God's wrath with a curse on his family that came to pass when Elah, his son and successor, was killed (along with the rest of his family) by Zimri, who was to succeed him. Zimri's reign lasted for a mercifully short seven days, enough time, though, to earn his very own set of curses from God. After him came Omri, who managed to sin more than all his predecessors, so he must have been an interesting fellow. He also made Samaria the capital city of the northern kingdom of Israel. Then came Ahab.

Ahab was a particular scoundrel, who *'did more evil in the eyes of the Lord than any of those before him' and 'did more to provoke the Lord, the God of Israel, to anger than did all the kings of Israel before him'* (1 Kings 16:30, 33). Much of this was due to his choice of wife. Jezebel was a foreigner and worshipped a variety of pagan gods. Ahab was totally dominated by his evil wife and together they dedicated the kingdom to the pagan god Baal. But God was to provide a 'thorn in their side' in the person of Elijah the prophet and a showdown was imminent. It came at Mount Carmel and we read of it in 1 Kings 18.

In the light corner we have the Lord God, Creator of the Universe, represented by Elijah the prophet. In the dark corner is Baal, represented by 450 'prophets'. The task – to set fire to a bull without the use of hands, matches or any human agency. First, the prophets of Baal ranted and raved for a full day to attract their god's attention, but to no avail. 'Perhaps he is asleep,' taunted Elijah. They failed and all eyes turned to Elijah. He milked the moment by drenching the altar with water, and then called down fire from heaven. It came and the people realised who was the *real* God of Israel. The 450 prophets of Baal were subsequently slaughtered. This could have been a defining moment, signalling a mass repentance and return to the God of Israel. But it wasn't: Jezebel wasn't going to let a setback like this slow her down and Elijah was forced to flee into exile.

It is important to note that although it tends to be the rulers who bring judgement on the land, it doesn't necessarily mean that the evil that they embody is fully characteristic of their people. We read in 1 Kings 19:18 that there was still a remnant of 7,000 in Israel whose knees had not bowed down to Baal. In all of biblical (and church) history there is always a faithful remnant who remain true to God, despite contrary pressures that might surround them.

Although we have concentrated on the conflict between Israel and its erstwhile brothers to the south, other nations were continuing to appear on the scene, driven by the ebb and flow of ambitious rulers and empires. One such person was Ben-Hadad of Syria, who attacked Israel (or Samaria, as it was also called at this time). As biblical history shows us time after time, God appoints other nations to punish His people when they go astray. Although Israel under Ahab was about as astray as you can get, this was not such an occasion: the Syrians were defeated. God, in His mercy, was using this episode to remind Israel exactly who was pulling the strings.

It didn't seem to do any good, as Ahab persisted in his sins, and so he finally met his end in battle. Because his death had been prophesied, he went in disguise, seeking to dodge his destiny. But he fell foul of a stray arrow between the sections of his armour and died in his chariot.

In 841 BC, King Jehu was the new king in Israel, ordained by a prophet and ordered to finally rid the earth of the house of Ahab on account of the sins of Jezebel. Jezebel met her end thrown out of the palace window by a pair of eunuchs, and so another royal dynasty went the way of Jeroboam and Baasha and a new one was created. Would this one be any better? 2 Kings 10:18 sets the tone for this man's rule: *'Ahab served Baal a little; Jehu will serve him much,'* he declared, signing his own death warrant in the process.

Israel carried on being cursed by a string of maniacal monarchs, each adding their misdemeanours to the pool of judgement that was growing and growing. That judgement had a name: Assyria.

Assyria had been one of the leading players in the Near East, but it had been too far east to trouble the folk of Israel and Judah. This was beginning to change during the reign of Jehu and later that of his son, Jehoahaz, a particularly nasty piece of work. God showed His displeasure with this latest wicked king of Israel by allowing the Syrians in the north to kick up some bother. Amazingly, Jehoahaz had the cheek to turn to God for help and, even more amazingly, God listened to his pleas and sent help. Although under increasingly imminent judgement, the rulers and people of Israel were able to call upon the Lord, who was still willing to listen to them despite their sins.

Jeroboam II was the grandson of Jehoahaz. Although he was just as wicked as his forbears, his reign saw the restoration of the northern borders of Israel. The people of Israel became very complacent and boastful about this, mistakenly believing that they were a nation under

God's blessing. The prophets Amos and Hosea quickly put them straight: '*The Sovereign Lord has sworn by himself – the Lord God Almighty declares: "I abhor the pride of Jacob and detest his fortresses; I will deliver up the city and everything in it"'* (Amos 6:8). *'Do not rejoice, O Israel; do not be jubilant like the other nations. For you have been unfaithful to your God; you love the wages of a prostitute at every threshing-floor'* (Hosea 9:1). The clock was ticking . . .

In Hosea 13:9–11 God proclaims the epitaph for the northern kingdom of Israel, reminding them that kings were what they demanded (back in the day of Samuel) and it was to be kings that brought their downfall: *'You are destroyed, O Israel, because you are against me, against your helper. Where is your king, that he may save you? Where are your rulers in all your towns, of whom you said, "Give me a king and princes"? So in my anger I gave you a king, and in my wrath I took him away.'*

The end came during the reign of Hoshea, the twentieth ruler, who came to the throne in 732 BC. Ironically, although he was evil, he hadn't sunk to the depths of some of his predecessors. Yet it was he who had to bear the full brunt of God's judgement. One day the Assyrians invaded, angry that Israel had made friends with Egypt, their bitter enemy. They imprisoned Hoshea and laid siege to the land. After three years (they were patient), the siege was over and the Israelites deported en masse to various locations in the Assyrian empire.

The northern kingdom of Israel was no more and the people largely vanished into obscurity, their memory kept alive by a multitude of myths about the 'lost tribes of Israel'. If God wants a people 'lost', then that's it, they're LOST. The northern kingdom simply went the way of the many peoples, like the Canaanites, Philistines and Moabites, who served their purpose in His plans but then disappear from the pages of history.

This is not to say that the ten tribes were totally lost – only those who were living in the northern kingdom at the time of the exile. Many had left earlier. Some remained in the southern kingdom when the nation first split (1 Kings 12:17). Some returned there a few years after the split (2 Chronicles 11:14–17). Others returned at various points, appalled at the growing apostasy of the northern kingdom. You can read about these in 2 Chronicles 15:9 and 2 Chronicles 30:25–26. The point I wish to make is that, when considering that the Jews are descended from the folk of the southern kingdom of Judah, it is safe to say that *all tribes* were represented among these people, not just Judah and Benjamin.

Deportation was a common fate for all who opposed the Assyrians. It was their way of discouraging revolt: the people deported first were the natural leaders. The deportation of the Israelites was fairly thorough and the area left behind became predominantly Gentile, though some Israelite land-workers remained. The northern part of this area was eventually to be renamed 'Galilee of the Gentiles'. The southern part, the area of Samaria, was to be resettled by other displaced folk, carted in from the far reaches of the Assyrian empire. These were eventually to become the mixed-race Samaritans of Jesus' day.

Why the mass deportation? Was it really because of the sin of King Jeroboam and his successors? The answer is given in 2 Kings 17. Verse 7 says '*All this took place because the Israelites had sinned against the Lord their God, who had brought them out of Egypt from under the power of Pharaoh king of Egypt.*' God's anger burned against both these evil rulers and their subjects for following the detestable practices of the other nations and ignoring the pleadings of prophets such as Elijah, Elisha, Amos and Hosea who were sent to warn them.

The whole sorry 'Israel' episode is summarised in 2 Kings 17:21, when God reminds us how it started and why it finished. How He tore Israel away from the house of David because of the sins of Solomon. How He gave this new kingdom to Jeroboam, promising him either blessings or curses, depending on his conduct. How Jeroboam's sin was even worse than Solomon's, bringing curses down upon himself and his family. How every subsequent king followed in his idolatry and unbelief, leading ultimately to the destruction and exile of the northern kingdom of Israel.

The future of God's people now rested with the southern kingdom of Judah, the Judeans – the *Jews*. Yes, this where the word comes from – people from the kingdom of Judah. As far as the promises given to Abraham by God are concerned, it's now up to the Jews, rather than the Israelites, to carry the banner of the covenant.

How do all these events line up with the covenants made with Abraham and Moses? As already mentioned, the covenant promises regarding the land were summed up in the Palestinian covenant. This warned God's people that the punishment for unfaithfulness and disobedience would be exile from the land, but the right to the land would *never* be taken from them and one day in the future it would be theirs again. What it *doesn't* promise is an easy ride, and if a large proportion of God's people, the Israelites from the northern kingdom, were to be pruned away, then so be it – at least there is a sizeable remnant, the Jews, left behind to inherit the land, however long this might take for a complete fulfilment. Of course, it would now be through the Jews that the other aspects of the covenant with Abraham would be fulfilled, including the future blessing of mankind in the person of the Messiah who was to come. We now turn our attention to the Jews, the people of the southern kingdom of Judah.

The kings of Judah were, on the whole, a better bunch than their Israel counterparts, with a liberal seasoning of good kings, though the first, Rehoboam, was weak and managed to lose the treasures of the temple and the royal palace to an Egyptian invader. This invasion severely weakened the kingdom and certainly didn't help them in dealing with the constant friction with the northern kingdom of Israel. Rehoboam's son Abijah was not much of an improvement, but Asa, the next in line, was.

Asa was the first good king of Judah. We read in 1 Kings 15:14 that *'Asa's heart was fully committed to the Lord all his life'*. He got rid of the idols that his predecessors had erected and even booted out his grandmother from a position of authority because of her pagan leanings.

His son Jehoshaphat, too, was a good 'un. He *'walked in the ways of his father Asa'* (1 Kings 22:43). Although he rid the land of the shrine-prostitutes, his eyes and ears weren't everywhere and there were still 'high places' in the kingdom where pagan sacrifices were made. He was succeeded, unfortunately, by a couple of bad kings, who managed to undo all the good achievements of their predecessors. The first was Jehoram, who sealed his fate by marrying the daughter of the weak King Ahab of Israel and his evil wife Jezebel. The second was Ahaziah, his son, who also married into Ahab's family and was a close buddy of Joram, the king of Israel. This was a big mistake, as when Joram was assassinated, the assassin saw off Ahaziah too, to complete the royal set.

Now here's a little known fact. One of the kings of Judah was, in fact, a queen! And a nasty one to boot, which is not surprising as Athaliah was the daughter of Jezebel! Yes, this was the queen mother who, on the death of her son Ahaziah, seized power by massacring the rest of her family, but she overlooked her six-month-old grandson Joash, who was whisked away and brought up in secrecy. It was the very stuff of fairy tales, particularly as later he was brought out of hiding and took the throne as a seven-year-old, at which point the evil Athaliah was done to death outside the temple walls.

Of course, a seven-year-old can't govern a country, so Joash was aided by Jehoiada the priest. This priest was a real man of God and rededicated the king and the people of Judah to God at a ceremony culminating with the tearing down of the temple of Baal and the killing of the pagan priest. The Lord's temple was then repaired, which was a good thing but unfortunately once Joash had come of age and outgrown the influence of Jehoiada, he went the way of the wicked. Eventually, in an attempt to forestall God's judgement, prophets came to Joash, warning of God's wrath. But he ignored them and went as far as killing one of them, Zechariah, who happened to be Jehoiada's son. As a result, Judah came under enemy attack and Joash was eventually assassinated by his own officials.

There is a continuing theme with God's treatment of the bad kings of Judah. Knowing that the Davidic line (i.e. the descendants of David) had to be kept intact both to preserve the Jewish people and to eventually produce the promised Messiah, God refused to turn His back on the people of Judah. We read of this in 2 Kings 8:19: *'Nevertheless, for the sake of his servant David, the Lord was not willing to destroy Judah. He had promised to maintain a lamp for David and his descendants for ever.'* Although there would be many setbacks along the way, the consequences of bad leadership, Judah would never go the way of Israel. It would survive on account of God's eternal plan for the Jews.

The next three kings of Judah – Amaziah, Azariah and Jotham – blew hot and cold. On the positive side they 'did what was right in the eyes of the Lord' (though not as well as David had done), but this was spoiled by the fact that the high places were not removed and unlawful sacrifices continued to be made. For his sins, Azariah seems to have been afflicted with leprosy for much of his reign.

We then arrive at Ahaz, son of Jotham, one of the worst kings of Judah. It was an understatement to say that *'he did not do what was right in the eyes of the Lord his God'* (2 Kings 16:2), as he not only offered unlawful sacrifices in high places but also sacrificed his own son to alien gods. This was the time of the Assyrians and their invasion of the northern kingdom of Israel was imminent. The king of Israel attempted to get Ahaz to help him in the fight against this common enemy and, when that failed, decided to invade Judah instead. This backfired as Ahaz went to Assyria for help, taking temple treasures with him to oil the deal and even going as far as to defile the temple with a pagan altar.

One man spoke out against this desecration and folly: the prophet Isaiah, who lived in Jerusalem at this time. Through him, God tried to calm Ahaz down, telling him just to trust in Him and all would be OK. Isaiah even offered a sign, which Ahaz refused. But Isaiah gave it anyway. It was the sign of Immanuel. These are verses in Isaiah 7:14 that we read at Christmas time, speaking of the virgin birth: *'Therefore the Lord himself will give you a sign: the virgin will be with child and will give birth to a son, and will call him Immanuel'*.

What have Ahaz and his problems got to do with the birth of Jesus? Actually, nothing directly. It is all to do with how we read and understand scripture. Up to now we have been looking at the plain literal sense of scripture as we build up the story of the Jews in the Old Testament. There seems to be no reason to change our approach here. The problem is that there have been arguments as to exactly what the literal meaning of this passage is! Which baby is being born (the child of Ahaz or Isaiah) and how do we explain a virgin birth in Old Testament times? There's no room here to investigate further but it's worth mentioning that the best fit for this particular verse is if we take it as a prophecy for the coming of Jesus the Messiah. And this is why we quote it at Christmas time.

As I said, Ahaz did not heed the wise words of Isaiah, and Judah became just one of many kingdoms that were self-administered but subservient to the Assyrian empire. But at least it was never conquered, mainly thanks to the next king of Judah, Hezekiah. Here was a really good king, one who even destroyed those high places. 2 Kings 18:5 tells us *'There was no-one like him among all the kings of Judah, either before him or after him.'*

The Assyrians were threatening, confident after their defeat of Israel in Hezekiah's sixth year. Eight years later, they came again and managed to capture many of the cities in Judah. Hezekiah was forced to send them treasure to pacify them and things didn't look good, but it was not God's plan for Judah to go the way of Israel, which was just as well because soon the huge Assyrian army was at the gates of Jerusalem. Hezekiah, being a godly king, consulted Isaiah, who told him not to worry as the Lord was with him. That night, the angel of the Lord killed 185,000 of the Assyrian invaders in their camp. The rest withdrew to Nineveh, their tails firmly between their legs, and their king, Sennacherib, was subsequently slaughtered by his sons, a fate predicted by Isaiah!

That was the Assyrian threat seen off, but a new threat was on the horizon. Babylon was stirring. The last conversation between Isaiah and Hezekiah concerned a 'friendly' visit from some Babylonian envoys. Isaiah warned him with these prophetic words: *'The time will surely come when everything in your palace, and all that your fathers have stored up until this day, will be carried off to Babylon. Nothing will be left, says the Lord. And some of your descendants, your own flesh and blood who will be born to you, will be taken away, and they will become eunuchs in the palace of the king of Babylon'* (Isaiah 39:6–7). Hezekiah's response was stoic and a little selfish: *'"The word of the Lord you have spoken is good," Hezekiah replied. For he thought, "There will be peace and security in my lifetime."'* He was a good king, so we'll forgive him!

It is hard to believe that the most godly king of Judah could have a son who was a complete horror, the most evil king of all. Manasseh was his name and this was his catalogue of shame in his 55-year reign. He rebuilt the high places and erected a variety of altars to pagan gods, even in the temple itself. He practised sorcery and divination and was responsible for the shedding of much innocent blood. God declared in 2 Kings 21:9 *'Manasseh led them astray, so that they did more evil than the nations the Lord had destroyed before the Israelites.'* God was angry and judgement was not far off now. He promises in verse 12, *'I am going to bring such disaster on Jerusalem and Judah that the ears of everyone who hears of it will tingle.'* The reason for God's extreme reaction was that Manasseh's reign was so long, his pagan measures had time to take root – to such an extent that only by having the slate wiped completely clean could the kingdom be rid of them.

Judgement was forestalled again by the actions of a righteous king. This was King Josiah, grandson of the evil Manasseh. One day the high priest was pottering about in the temple, in the middle of a rebuilding campaign, when he discovered a book. It was the Book of the Law, probably a copy of the Book of Deuteronomy. It was read out to Josiah, who was shocked to discover how far God's people had fallen from the standards set out in scripture and how judgement was imminent. Josiah had to act quickly and had the book read out aloud at a meeting of the great and the good (and the bad) of the land. By doing so, he rededicated his people to God and, in return for this, was told *'Your eyes will not see all the disaster I am going to bring on this place'* (2 Kings 22:20).

He then embarked on a thorough campaign to undo the harm that his father and, particularly, his grandfather had done to the kingdom. He tore down shrines, Asherah poles and altars and killed pagan priests, mediums and spiritualists. Passover was celebrated for the first time since the times of the judges.

Josiah didn't act alone; he had the counsel of a couple of God's top prophets. Zephaniah was a real encourager of the king and no doubt had a hand in many of the reforms. Jeremiah was just starting his ministry at this time. He, too, encouraged Josiah in his reforms, but he knew that however hard the king might try, the heart of the people was not right and there was a big difference between outward observances and inner convictions. Such was the legacy of Manasseh.

In 2 Kings 23:25 we read that *'neither before nor after Josiah was there a king like him who turned to the Lord as he did – with all his heart and with all his soul and with all his strength, in accordance with all the Law of Moses'.* Yet in the very next verse we encounter the sober reality that judgement was forestalled, not averted: *'Nevertheless, the Lord did not turn away from the heat of his fierce anger, which burned against Judah because of all that Manasseh had done to provoke him to anger. So the Lord said, "I will remove Judah also from my presence as I removed Israel, and I will reject Jerusalem, the city I chose, and this temple, about which I said, 'There shall my Name be.'"'*

After Josiah came the evil Jehoahaz, who thankfully only lasted three months. He was followed by Jehoiakim, who was little better, followed by a further tongue-twister, Jehoiachin (also known as Jeconiah), who also carried on the family traditions! Jeremiah knew that a national calamity was not far off and he spent no little time proclaiming this unpopular message. He had a special word for this latest king and it was no word of comfort! In Jeremiah 22:24, 30 we read *'"As surely as I live," declares the Lord, "even if you, Jehoiachin son of Jehoiakim king of Judah, were a signet ring on my right hand, I would still pull you off . . . Record this man as if childless, a man who will not prosper in his lifetime, for none of his off-spring will prosper, none will sit on the throne of David or rule any more in Judah."'*

This is awesome stuff because the Lord, through Jeremiah, declares that no descendant of Jehoiachin (Jeconiah) will sit on the throne of David. Although he's not the first king to be so cursed, he's the only one to be mentioned in the genealogy of the Messiah in Matthew 1! Surely this means that if Jesus is descended from this man then he couldn't be the promised one, the Christ, because Jeconiah's line has been cursed? True, but if you look closely at this genealogy in Matthew 1:2–16, you'll see that it is the genealogy of Joseph, husband of Mary. Jeconiah was Joseph's ancestor, but not Jesus' ancestor if we accept that Joseph was not the father of Jesus. Now we are reminded of that verse we read earlier, Isaiah 7:14: *'Therefore the LORD himself will give you a sign: The virgin will be with child and will give birth to a son, and will call him Immanuel.'* It's fun when the Bible makes so much sense and explains itself so elegantly, isn't it?

It was now over ten years since the death of the godly Josiah and despite all his reforms, the ungodly practices had yet again returned big time. Prophets might as well have been banging their heads against brick walls. Jeremiah went as far as to proclaim the sacred temple as something now cursed by God because of the sins of the people. This put him on trial for blasphemy, but he got off on a technicality – how could someone proven as God's spokesman be speaking blasphemy?

While all this was happening, the Babylonians came, saw and conquered. Daniel the prophet is quite matter-of-fact about what happened in 605 BC. *'In the third year of the reign of Jehoiakim king of Judah, Nebuchadnezzar king of Babylon came to Jerusalem and besieged it. And the Lord delivered Jehoiakim king of Judah into his hand, along with some of the articles from the temple of God. These he carried off to the temple of his god in Babylonia and put in the treasure-house of his god'* (Daniel 1:1–2). Daniel was one of a group of noblemen carted off to Babylon at that time.

This wasn't the main event and Jeremiah proclaimed it quite bluntly. *'So Jeremiah the prophet said to all the people of Judah and to all those living in Jerusalem: For twenty-three years – from the thirteenth year of Josiah son of Amon king of Judah until this very day – the word of the LORD has come to me and I have spoken to you again and again, but you have not listened. And though the Lord has sent all his ser-*

vants the prophets to you again and again, you have not listened or paid any attention. They said, "Turn now, each of you, from your evil ways and your evil practices, and you can stay in the land the Lord gave to you and your fathers for ever and ever. Do not follow other gods to serve and worship them; do not provoke me to anger with what your hands have made. Then I will not harm you." "But you did not listen to me," declares the LORD, *"and you have provoked me with what your hands have made, and you have brought harm to yourselves." Therefore the Lord Almighty says this: "Because you have not listened to my words, I will summon all the peoples of the north and my servant Nebuchadnezzar king of Babylon,"* declares the LORD, *"and I will bring them against this land and its inhabitants and against all the surrounding nations. I will completely destroy them and make them an object of horror and scorn, and an everlasting ruin. I will banish from them the sounds of joy and gladness, the voices of bride and bridegroom, the sound of millstones and the light of the lamp. This whole country will become a desolate wasteland, and these nations will serve the king of Babylon for seventy years"'* (Jeremiah 25:2–11).

So it happened. The temple and most of Jerusalem was burned down and the people of the city, indeed the cream of the rest of Judah – priests, craftsmen, the wealthy etc. – were led into exile, mostly to Babylon itself. The other, mostly poorer, folk were left behind to work the vineyards and the fields. Jeremiah, for his pains, was slung into prison.

The difference between this exile of Judah and the earlier exile of Israel is important. Israel was dispersed to a variety of places and, for all intents and purposes, left the story. Judah was largely deported, as a whole, to one place, Babylon. They kept their identity, as Judeans, or Jews, and this is demonstrated very ably in the Book of

Daniel, which was written totally in a Babylonian context.

The Promised Land was now only sparsely populated, with refugees from elsewhere in the Assyrian empire in the north and poor farmers in the south. Jews were still in the land, but with the smallest population since the heady days of Joshua and the Israelites.

Again, we must consider these events in the light of God's covenants with Abraham and Moses. I remind you that the covenant promises regarding the land were summed up in the Palestinian covenant, warning the Jews that the punishment for unfaithfulness and disobedience would be exile from the land, but that the right to the land would never be taken from them and one day in the future it would be theirs again.

The Israelites of the northern kingdom had already been exiled, with no hope of return, but when the Jews of the southern kingdom now largely go into exile too, they are reminded that their exile is to be temporary, in fact just 70 years, as we read in Jeremiah 25. Even Isaiah, who had died over a century earlier, spoke of this in Isaiah 48:12–22: *'Leave Babylon, flee from the Babylonians! Announce this with shouts of joy and proclaim it'* (verse 20). The great prophet of the exile was Ezekiel and he too reminded the Jews of a return to the land, but he mysteriously spoke more about *another* return, one that was far off in the future. More of that later.

It is worth mentioning that since the northern kingdom had disappeared from the scene a couple of centuries earlier, the name *Israel* is now used to refer to the Jews, who are mainly languishing in parts of the Babylonian empire. The Book of Ezekiel, written to the Jews in exile, uses the word 'Israel' 158 times and doesn't mention the word 'Jews' once. We should note

that from now on the words 'Israel' and 'Jews' are referring to the same people, lest other groups start to claim
the name Israel for themselves.

The Jews in Babylonia were sorely tempted. Their
exile must have been a wrenching experience but their
new home had its 'plus points'. After all, Babylonia was
one of the most ostentatiously rich empires the world
has seen and this must have been a striking contrast to
the austerity and restrictions back in Judah. Many were
won over by these riches and, like the Israelites earlier,
disappear from the pages of our story. Others wept by
the river of Babylon. Psalm 137 tells us that there was a
faithful remnant who yearned for the 'good old days':
*'By the rivers of Babylon we sat and wept when we remem-
bered Zion . . . How can we sing the songs of the Lord while in
a foreign land? If I forget you, O Jerusalem, may my right
hand forget its skill. May my tongue cling to the roof of my
mouth if I do not remember you, if I do not consider Jerusalem
my highest joy.'* These were God's people, the faithful
remnant who were going to ensure that His covenant
would remain intact – after all, if *all* of the Jews had been
assimilated into the Babylonian culture, then that would
have been that – no Jews, no Messiah, no Jesus!

Empires come and empires go and the mighty
Babylonian empire wasn't to last long. Within 50 years,
Babylon itself had fallen to the Medes and Persians and,
on the order of Cyrus in the sixth century BC, Jewish
exiles were allowed back into their land, along with the
captured temple treasures. Why did he do it? This
seemed an odd act from a leader of a mighty empire. The
answer is given in Ezra 1:2–3 and it shows who really is
the 'boss of history'. It reads *'This is what Cyrus king of
Persia says: "The LORD, the God of heaven, has given me all
the kingdoms of the earth and he has appointed me to build a*

temple for him at Jerusalem in Judah. Anyone of his people among you – may his God be with him and let him go up to Jerusalem in Judah and build the temple of the Lord, the God of Israel, the God who is in Jerusalem."'

The first trickle back to the land was led by Zerubbabel, for the express purpose of rebuilding the temple in Jerusalem, according to the wishes of Cyrus, confirmed by the Word of God through the prophets Haggai and Zechariah. Zerubbabel was chosen specially for this task, as we read in Haggai 2:23: '"*On that day," declares the Lord Almighty, "I will take you, my servant Zerubbabel son of Shealtiel," declares the Lord, "and I will make you like my signet ring, for I have chosen you," declares the Lord Almighty.' Zechariah confirms the task he has been selected for. 'The hands of Zerubbabel have laid the foundation of this temple; his hands will also complete it. Then you will know that the Lord Almighty has sent me to you'* (Zechariah 4:9). This man was special indeed, as Luke 3:27 tells us that he was one of the illustrious ancestors of Jesus, through the line of both Joseph and Mary.

This second temple (Solomon's temple being the first) was completed in 516 BC and it took 20 years to build. A reason for this late completion date was the opposition to the rebuilding by the Samaritans. They were the majority in the land at the time and wanted to keep it that way, so they would do anything to keep Jewish observances to a minimum.

Sixty years later Ezra the priest, accompanied by around 2,000 other Jews, was sent from Babylonia to Judah. The reason was to whip the Jewish population into shape, religiously speaking, as a decline had set in since the days of Zerubbabel. Ezra seems to have been given the responsibility of spiritual advisor to the nation and he had a real job on his hands getting the people right with God, particularly as there had been much intermarriage with the other nations. He led the people into repentance and revival, helped later by Nehemiah, who was a Jew living in Susa employed as the cupbearer to the Persian king of the day. Nehemiah heard that the Jewish community in Jerusalem was in great distress and he was given a commission to rebuild the walls of the city. He became governor of the land, a post that he held for 12 years – a marked contrast to his earlier career and an encouragement to all of us with talents so hidden that only God can coax them out of us. Nehemiah's story is told in the biblical book of his name.

A decade later Nehemiah was recalled to Babylon and, in his absence, the people fell into their old ways – intermarriage, corruption and the like. Malachi was the latest prophet sent by God to warn and chastise His people. He was to be the last prophet of the Old Testament.

We may have reached the end of the Old Testament, but we have certainly not escaped from its influence and reach. As well as the history, poetry and teachings, we must not forget that much of the Old Testament was prophecy. Some of it was fulfilled during Old Testament times, particularly the warnings concerning the exile and the subsequent return from Babylon. Yet much of it remained unfulfilled. Three major themes dominate this unfulfilled prophecy: the coming of Jesus, the restoration of Israel and the end times.

The first of these to be (partly) fulfilled was when Jesus arrived on the scene some four centuries later. The rest of the prophecies – concerned with Jesus' second coming, the restoration of Israel and the end times – had many more centuries to wait before coming to pass.

Of these prophecies, the most contentious are those regarding the restoration of Israel. Is the modern State of

Israel a fulfilment of biblical prophecy or just a historical oddity and a political embarrassment?

The way we approach these particular prophecies is crucial to our honest dealings with the Word of God. We are not talking of a few ambiguous prophetic utterances; we are talking of scores of prophecies from the mouths of most of the Old Testament prophets. As a taster of a fuller discussion later in this book, here are a few biblical references to whet your appetite: ~~Amos 9:14–15~~; Deuteronomy 30:3–5; Ezekiel 20:34; Ezekiel 34:13; Ezekiel 36:24; Genesis 28:10–15; Isaiah 27:12–13; Isaiah 43:5–6; Jeremiah 23:3–6; Jeremiah 32:36–41; Zechariah 8:7–8; Amos 9:14–15; Ezekiel 4:3–6; Ezekiel 11:17; Ezekiel 37:10–14; Micah 7:8–11; Jeremiah 32:44; Jeremiah 16:14–15; Isaiah 66:7–8; Jeremiah 31:35–36.

We have now come to the end of our Old Testament review of the Jews in their land, first in Canaan at the time of the Exodus, then as Israel and Judah, and finally as a remote outpost of the Assyrian, Babylonian and Persian empires. But at no point was this not God's land. In Leviticus 25:23 we read, *'the land is mine and you are but aliens and my tenants'*. Even the mighty Cyrus knew this when he stated that God was 'in Jerusalem'. It was God's land then as it is now, but it is also covenant land and although the tenants may have occasionally been forced to sub-let, everyone who lives in His land does so only by permission from the Author of History, for His purposes.

Chapter 4

Judea and Samaria

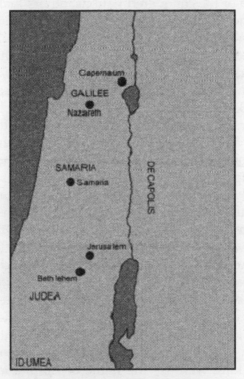

Fig. 5: **Roman Occupation**

Have you ever wondered why the New Testament was written in Greek at a time when the country was populated by Jews speaking Hebrew and Aramaic and governed by Latin-speaking Romans? For an answer, we have to rejoin our history of Israel at the point when God goes strangely quiet, as far as scripture is concerned. He seemingly enters into a 450-year slumber, perhaps carefully planning His comeback in the person of Jesus the Messiah.

Empires come and go, some making major changes to the culture of the conquered nations, others making little impact. The Ancient Greeks made a real impact and, in many ways, still influence our current thinking. First they enlightened the world in the areas of philosophy, mathematics and science with such luminaries as Aristotle, Socrates and Plato, then they conquered it, spreading not only their knowledge but also their culture and language. Alexander the Great was responsible for the latter. Described as probably the greatest military genius of all time, he conquered territories as far apart as India in the east and Egypt in the south. In the middle was little old Judea and Samaria, smarting from its third conquest in three turbulent centuries, passing from Persian to Greek hands after the defeat of the Persian empire in 331 BC.

At that time, it was just a province of the Greek empire. Actually, it fell within the Seleucid empire, named after Seleucus, one of the two generals who succeeded Alexander. The most significant event of those times was during the reign of Antiochus IV. He was the latest in a line of kings called Seleucus and Antiochus, a succession expedited by a series of strategic poisonings. This new king went by the name of Epiphanes, which meant 'God made manifest'. He obviously had a high opinion of himself, which wasn't shared by the Jews of the day. They renamed him Epimanes, a play on words meaning 'completely barmy'. He was hated by those

Jews who were eager to preserve their heritage in the face of the Greece-ifying or Hellenization that was going on. His aim was to erase Judaism forever and to turn all the Jews into Greeks. He did this craftily, by passing laws punishable by death for anyone practising Judaism, keeping the Sabbath or even found in possession of sacred scrolls. In every town and village, altars were set up to Greek gods, and sport – dedicated to these gods – was made a major part of life.

The last straw for those Jews who still clung to their beliefs was in 168 BC. Antiochus' soldiers brought a statue of Zeus into the temple in Jerusalem and sacrificed a pig on the altar. This was the ultimate insult to God-fearing Jews and provoked a national stirring, leading to the uprising led by Judas the Maccabee. When the (eventually) victorious Judas and his men entered the temple in Jerusalem they found it in total disarray and defiled by the altar and the idol. They destroyed all that was impure and rededicated the temple to God. This is commemorated by Jews to this day at Hanukkah, the Festival of Dedication.

These were important historical events because there was a real danger that the Jews would have been assimilated into Greek culture, with the same end result as when the northern kingdom of Israel was absorbed into the Assyrian empire and lost to history centuries before. God would not allow this to happen, for the sake of His covenant with Abraham regarding the land as an everlasting possession for His people the Jews, His covenant with David (2 Samuel 7:11–16) promising a 'seed of David' to inherit an eternal kingdom, and His promise through Jeremiah (Jeremiah 31:31–34) of a new covenant written on people's hearts.

How could a Jewish Messiah be born (and recognised as such) if all Jews had become assimilated and had

swapped synagogues for gymnasia and the Torah for
Aristotle? God had to act and He did so through such
people as the Maccabees and the many martyrs who
died for their faith at that time. The Jewish people had to
prevail, the Messianic line of David had to be preserved,
as we read in Jeremiah 23:5–6: *'"The days are coming,"
declares the* LORD, *"when I will raise up to David a righteous
Branch, a King who will reign wisely and do what is just and
right in the land. In his days Judah will be saved and Israel
will live in safety. This is the name by which he will be called:
The* LORD *Our Righteousness."'*

In 161 BC, Judas the Maccabee was killed in battle, two
years after his brother Eleazar had met an untimely end
crushed by an elephant (after spearing it in the stomach
from below!), also in battle. From Judas a fam-ily
dynasty was created, the Hasmonean dynasty, the name
coming from Hashmon, a distant ancestor. From this
time onwards for a hundred years, thanks to a peace
treaty forged by another brother, Simon, Judea and
Samaria remained more or less an independent state,
ruled by a convoluted succession of Hasmoneans. These
rulers also generally functioned as high priests in an
intriguing mixture of the sacred and the secular. Simon
was a benevolent ruler, easy on any Jews who had been
Hellenized, and was held in such high esteem that he
was not only the ruler and high priest, but was also
given the role of commander-in-chief of the army!
Interestingly he was made hereditary high priest 'until
such time as God speaks to the contrary'. As it was then
believed that prophecy had ceased in Israel, this was
expected to last forever. As history was soon to show,
they were wrong on both counts!

Under the Hasmoneans, Jewish territory expanded
from the small state of Judea, roughly equivalent to the

territory held by the tribe of Judah, to take in territory after territory under subsequent rulers. Eventually the land also included much that was part of the old empire of Solomon, back in the days before the exile. On the religious front, there had always been people, notably the Hassids, who opposed the idea of the Hasmonean rulers also functioning as high priests. This came to a head around 100 BC with the emergence of the Pharisees, a national religious revivalist movement who, despite their later bad press, were actually a breath of fresh air at the time. In many ways, they represented the ancient equivalent of the Christian charismatic revival at the end of the twentieth century. The Pharisees opposed the status quo of the hereditary priesthood but they were opposed in turn by another new group, the Sadducees, who were in support of the priesthood. Many battles were fought between these factions in the Sanhedrin, the religious ruling body. It seems that the scene was being firmly set for the events to come in the Gospels, but there were a few more glitches to overcome first.

Things started to get fraught through the actions of the third generation of Hasmoneans. The first of this generation, Aristobulus, called himself king, killed his mother and one brother and threw his other brothers in prison. He was succeeded by one of these brothers, Alexander Jannaeus (a name combining Greek elements with Hebrew), who turned out even worse. Under his rule, the Pharisees organised an uprising which he put down by crucifying 800 souls after slaughtering their wives and children before their eyes. Although he was responsible for a great expansion of the kingdom he was, unsurprisingly, deeply unpopular with his Jewish subjects. His way of life was more Greek than Hebrew and the thought of a high priest with so much blood on his hands was too much to bear. Something had to give and it did, with the coming of the Romans in 63 BC.

The Roman general Pompey took Jerusalem that year, slaughtering some 12,000 Jews in the process – a tragic pattern set at the time of the Babylonians but sadly not to end there, as history will bear evidence. The Romans were on a conquering tour of the Middle East and decided to intervene in a dispute between two Hasmonean brothers, Hyrcanus II and Aristobulus II, who were fighting for control. Rome favoured Hyrcanus over the cunning Aristobulus and so the latter was thrown into jail, while the former was given the throne of Judea.

But there were strings attached, as this brought the whole land under indirect Roman rule as a province of Syria. A generation later, Roman influence was brought to bear through the selection of a new king for the province, King Herod. Identified as someone who could further Roman influence in the east, Herod was declared the 'King of the Jews' by the emperor and sent off to conquer the land. After a three-year campaign, Jerusalem yet again came under siege and, after it was taken, Herod sent his vanquished opponent, the hapless Antigonus, off to Rome to be beheaded.

King Herod reigned for 33 years and was deeply unpopular. The main reason was his use of the title 'King of the Jews', which rankled as he was really descended from the Edomites. These were traditional enemies of the Jews who had been forcibly 'Judaised' a couple of generations back. He tried to alleviate this by marrying a Hasmonean princess after divorcing his previous wife Doris. His new mother-in-law was a battleaxe who forced him to install his brother-in-law Aristobulus as high priest. Unfortunately, Aristobulus was drowned after high jinks in a swimming pool (serves him right as high priests were not meant to frolic about!), which had international repercussions, particularly with Cleopatra of Egypt (yes, it was she), who had her eyes on expansion eastwards. She had Herod summoned to her friend Mark Antony to account for himself, which he did with a large bribe. The purpose of recounting this episode is that this was the point when Herod started to develop a deeply suspicious nature which, as the Gospels and the Acts of the Apostles attest, was to sink into eventual madness.

Yet Herod did some good: He brought peace to the north-eastern territories and he loved building things. With the help of a thousand burly Levites, he built a new temple in Jerusalem to add to the one he had built for the Roman emperor in Samaria. He also built stadiums and theatres, although this didn't make him too popular as they were intended for the forthcoming Greek games. He gave Roman names to the local regions and towns, some of them in honour of his own family, even though he was to try to murder most of them in time.

Herod's temple took more than 80 years to build and the final trimmings were in place barely seven years before its destruction! Nevertheless, the temple was just about operational when it witnessed something significant and unusual in about 7 BC (or in 1 BC for traditionalists). An elderly priest, Zechariah, had a meeting with the angel Gabriel there while on a tour of duty. Subsequently, his wife Elizabeth was to give birth to a son, John. John the Baptist was to grow up to be very special indeed. We read of him in Matthew 3:3: '*This is he who was spoken of through the prophet Isaiah: "A voice of one calling in the desert, 'Prepare the way for the Lord, make straight paths for him.'"*' God's apparent silence was over. More than 400 years after Malachi, the last prophet of the Hebrew scriptures, we now have a new voice, that of John the Baptist, and we move to the world of the Gospels.

King Herod died a madman, one of his last acts being to order the slaughter of all infants in the Bethlehem area after discovering the presence of a rival 'King of the Jews'. This, of course, was Jesus, the true King of the Jews, who by now had escaped to Egypt. After Herod's death, his kingdom was split into three and given to his three sons, none taking the title of king. Herod Antipas became a tetrarch (a minor title) and ruled Galilee, falling foul of John the Baptist in Matthew 14:1–12. Archelaus became the much more politically important ethnarch of Judea, which did him little good as, after a few bad decisions, he was banished to Europe. From this time on Judea was proclaimed a province of the Roman empire and was governed by a Roman official, a procurator, appointed by the emperor. The fifth such procurator was Pontius Pilate, who governed from AD 26 to AD 36.

By now the Roman hold on the province was firm. The heart of the country was Judea in the south and Galilee in the north, separated by Samaria, which was inhabited by a people who were not quite 'kosher', with a religion that tended to 'mix-and-match' the Judaism of the day, which was not surprising as they were descended from immigrants from the Assyrian empire. Jerusalem at that time was a splendid place, the most dazzling sight being that of the temple. There may have been as many as 250,000 people living there at the time, swelling to millions during the pilgrim festivals. Local affairs were sorted out by the Sanhedrin, but real power was held by the Romans. All major decisions had to be referred to the Roman authorities, including the death sentence on Jesus, which had to be approved by Pilate.

The people had high expectations of Jesus of Nazareth, Yeshua ben Yosef. He was the one about whom John the Baptist, his cousin, had spoken. He was the Lord, the anointed one, the Messiah. His identity was woven throughout the fabric of the Hebrew scriptures; he was the promised one of the House of David. You could say that all of the history of Israel up to that point, even the bad stuff, was guided by heavenly strings so that the Son could be born into such an environment at such a time. God had this in mind when, 2,000 years earlier, He made His covenant with Abraham, promising the possession of the land and also spiritual benefits to come. For all the subsequent years, God nurtured the Messianic line, from Abraham, Isaac and Jacob through to David and onwards, surviving invasions by Assyrians, Babylonians, Persians, Greeks and Romans. If Jewish survival itself was a minor miracle, the preservation of this promised line, as listed in the genealogies in Matthew 1 and Luke 3, was a major one indeed!

So we now reach the Christian age, the New Covenant prophesied by Jeremiah: *"'The time is coming," declares the Lord, "when I will make a new covenant with the house of Israel and with the house of Judah. It will not be like the covenant I made with their forefathers when I took them by the hand to lead them out of Egypt, because they broke my covenant, though I was a husband to them," declares the Lord. "This is the covenant that I will make with the house of Israel after that time," declares the Lord. "I will put my law in their minds and write it on their hearts. I will be their God, and they will be my people"'* (Jeremiah 31:31–33).

So how does this fit in with our understanding of God's covenants?

The New Covenant instituted by the Lord Jesus through his sacrifice at the cross, was, as we read, primarily with the Jews. This makes us prick up our ears and consider how it relates to the two other covenants we have encountered in the Old Testament, the covenant with Abraham and the covenant with Moses.

The New Covenant *replaces* the one made with Moses, on account of the Jews breaking that particular covenant.

'But the ministry Jesus has received is as superior to theirs as the covenant of which he is mediator is superior to the old one, and it is founded on better promises. For if there had been nothing wrong with that first covenant, no place would have been sought for another. But God found fault with the people and said: "The time is coming, declares the Lord, when I will make a new covenant with the house of Israel and with the house of Judah. It will not be like the covenant I made with their forefathers when I took them by the hand to lead them out of Egypt, because they did not remain faithful to my covenant, and I turned away from them, declares the Lord. This is the covenant I will make with the house of Israel after that time, declares the Lord. I will put my laws in their minds and write them on their hearts. I will be their God, and they will be my people. No longer will a man teach his neighbour, or a man his brother, saying, 'Know the Lord,' because they will all know me, from the least of them to the greatest. For I will forgive their wickedness and will remember their sins no more." By calling this covenant 'new', he has made the first one obsolete; and what is obsolete and ageing will soon disappear' (Hebrews 8:6–13).*

We have to be clear about what is happening here. The covenant with Moses made at Sinai was a conditional covenant, which could be broken and was broken through the idolatrous and unfaithful behaviour of the Jews towards their God. This was the Mosaic covenant, replaced by the New Covenant instituted by Jesus.

So the covenant with Moses was no more, but the covenant with Abraham – which, as explained earlier, was unconditional – *remained intact*. It couldn't be broken and it wasn't broken. What this means is that the coming of Jesus would have no effect on the covenant with Abraham, although his coming did fulfil an aspect of the covenant. After all, Jesus was, without a doubt, the means by which *'all peoples on earth will be blessed'*. But this was just one aspect of the covenant – what about the others? God's promises to Abraham concerning the land are still in effect. Jesus' coming affected this not one jot. *'The whole land of Canaan, where you are now an alien, I will give as an everlasting possession to you and your descendants after you; and I will be their God'* (Genesis 17:8).

Misunderstandings on this point, and on the teaching of Jesus on the nature of his kingdom, lead some to go as far as to imply that he said 'Because I have come to initiate a new kingdom, this old talk of physical return to the land is now irrelevant'. Mr Shoots would say that Jesus' silence on the subject indicated that the land promises given to Abraham are no longer physical promises to the Jewish nation but *spiritual* promises to Christians. For them, the 'Promised Land' now becomes the *kingdom of heaven*.

If you followed this approach, you'd have to concede that Jesus was only interested in subjects that he explicitly taught about. Does this mean that, because Jesus didn't speak on child sacrifice (a practice totally condemned in the Old Testament), he was in fact saying that this was of no concern to him and it was OK to toss your children onto Molech's fiery altar? Common sense tells me that you can't formulate doctrine out of what is *not* spoken about!

The reason why Jesus did not speak about the land and God's promises of it to the Jews is that the New Covenant was to run alongside the one given to

Abraham, not instead of it, and so there was nothing new for him to add. The Abrahamic covenant was a given, a done deal, no arguments needed. Surely this fits the facts best – unless we *need* to believe that God's eternal promises to the Jews were torn up when Jesus appeared on the scene.

Why would people *need* to believe this? Because the alternative, for some, is not acceptable. It would imply a future for the Jewish people in the 'Promised Land', according to the plans of God.

If Jesus had intended to be radical enough to cancel an 'eternal' covenant, he certainly wouldn't have been silent about it. It would have been a key teaching, expounded in a clear and unambiguous way. There would have been no doubt where he stood on the matter. 'Verily, listen to me,' he would have said, 'I have come to tell you that the covenant God made with Abraham has now been fulfilled. He who follows me shall inherit the land . . .' But he said nothing of the sort; neither did he allude to it, hint at it or imply it!

Although Jesus wasn't too forthcoming, Paul *was*. In his letter to the Romans he said '*Theirs is the adoption as sons; theirs the divine glory, the covenants, the receiving of the law, the temple worship and the promises*' (Romans 9:4). Who was he writing about? The Jews. And which covenants was he writing about? God's covenants with the Jews, of course. As far as Paul was concerned, the covenants were still valid – as were, at the time of Paul's writing, all the other items listed.

It is worth having a quick view of some New Testament scriptures that Mr Shoots would use to back up his views.

He would look at Matthew 21:33–46, the Parable of the Tenants, and quote verse 43: '*Therefore I tell you that the kingdom of God will be taken away from you and given to a people who will produce its fruit.'* He would conclude that this shows Jesus rejecting the Jews as a 'chosen people'. If we carry on reading, to verse 45, we see that Jesus is *not* talking about the Jews as a people, he is speaking directly to the Jewish leadership, the chief priests and the Pharisees. In fact, this parable, as with others, speaks to all in positions of authority, reminding them of their responsibilities and the outcome of disobedience. It could equally speak to us if we are in positions of leadership.

He would look at Galatians 3:26–29: *'You are all sons of God through faith in Christ Jesus, for all of you who were baptised into Christ have clothed yourselves with Christ. There is neither Jew nor Greek, slave nor free, male nor female, for you are all one in Christ Jesus. If you belong to Christ, then you are Abraham's seed, and heirs according to the promise.'* He would point to this and say that surely there is no difference between Jew and Gentile any more. That's true, as far as *personal salvation* is concerned, through the New Covenant of Jesus the Messiah. When it comes to this issue, it is true that there are no differences between Jew and Greek – both equally need Jesus as Messiah. Jews have no fast track to heaven! The context of this verse, in fact the whole book, is that *non-Jews* can be saved, as well as Jews, and that the *spiritual blessings* of the Abrahamic covenant are for all to enjoy. If you take this verse as meaning that there is no longer any distinction between Jew and Greek, then you must equally say the same about men and women, or slave and free.

He would look at Hebrews 8:1–6: *'The point of what we are saying is this: We do have such a high priest, who sat down at the right hand of the throne of the Majesty in heaven, and who serves in the sanctuary, the true tabernacle set up by the*

Lord, not by man. Every high priest is appointed to offer both gifts and sacrifices, and so it was necessary for this one also to have something to offer. If he were on earth, he would not be a priest, for there are already men who offer the gifts prescribed by the law. They serve at a sanctuary that is a copy and shadow of what is in heaven. This is why Moses was warned when he was about to build the tabernacle: "See to it that you make everything according to the pattern shown you on the mountain." But the ministry Jesus has received is as superior to theirs as the covenant of which he is mediator is superior to the old one, and it is founded on better promises.' All this does is speak of the superiority of the New Covenant of Jesus over the Old Covenant with Moses. It is not concerned with the *older* covenant with Abraham and so these verses are irrelevant to our discussion.

He would *not* spend too much time on Romans 9–11, which explains exactly what God thinks of the Jewish people in the light of the New Covenant with Jesus. Read it for yourself and spend some time in a reliable commentary on these verses. Whole books have been written on these three chapters and it is unlikely that Mr Shoots would have paid them much attention. More on these chapters a little later.

About a week before his crucifixion, Jesus was approaching Jerusalem and started weeping. He gave his reason in Luke 19:42: *'If you, even you, had only known on this day what would bring you peace – but now it is hidden from your eyes. The days will come upon you when your enemies will build an embankment against you and encircle you and hem you in on every side. They will dash you to the ground, you and the children within your walls. They will not leave one stone on another, because you did not recognise the time of God's coming to you.'* It was a prophecy about the future, a prophecy that would be fulfilled within the lifetime of many who were listening. A few days later he spoke again about Jerusalem, his words recorded in Luke 21:20: *'When you see Jerusalem being surrounded by armies, you will know that its desolation is near. Then let those who are in Judea flee to the mountains, let those in the city get out, and let those in the country not enter the city.'*

What was going to happen, and why was it going to happen? Jesus answers in the very next sentence: *'For this is the time of punishment in fulfilment of all that has been written.'* More punishment: can't they get anything right? Well the fact is that the situation was a complex one, but the crux of it was that, for various reasons, the majority of Jews, particularly the leadership, failed to recognise Jesus as the promised Messiah. This was a major sin and one to have very serious repercussions. But back to our history lesson.

Pilate was recalled to Rome in AD 36, the same year that Herod Antipas suffered a heavy defeat in battle, followed by a falling out with the Romans. Next in line for control was Herod Agrippa, made King of Galilee and Judea by the crazy emperor Caligula in Rome. Meanwhile, in AD 40, there was trouble a-brewing in western Judea. Some Gentiles had erected an altar in the emperor's honour, which was torn down by God-fearing Jews. Caligula retaliated by insisting that his statue should be erected in the temple itself, in Jerusalem – shades of Antiochus Epiphanes! Thanks to an urgent intervention by Agrippa, Caligula relented. Shortly afterwards he was assassinated by the Roman authorities, who couldn't find a constitutional way of getting rid of such a maniac.

But the whole episode made Jews, particularly the growing band who put their faith in the resurrected Jesus of Nazareth, very nervous indeed. Herod Agrippa was no friend of these people; in fact, he was beginning to persecute them. He put James the apostle to death and threw Simon Peter into prison. We read of these things in Acts 12. Herod came to a grisly end though – being eaten by worms (verse 23) – after proclaiming himself a god in the deranged tradition of the Roman emperors.

The king is dead, long live the procurator – yes, we were now back to direct rule from Rome. The first was Fadus, who was succeeded in AD 46 by Alexander, a Jew who had abandoned the faith of his fathers. This was the time of a severe famine in the land, which we read of in Acts 11:27–30, with Paul and Barnabas organising relief efforts. In the next few years the Jews were becoming less and less pleased with the Roman occupying army, who cared little for the religious sensibilities of the natives, particularly as, unlike other conquered people, they stubbornly clung to their God and refused to have anything to do with the Roman deities. A growing band of Jewish rebels, springing from the zealot movement in Jesus' day, was now roaming the countryside, not averse to an occasional assassination of pro-Roman Jews.

The high priesthood had become heavily compromised and had become the property of a few Sadducean families. The actions of one of these, Ananias, at the trial of Paul before the Sanhedrin, can be read in Acts 23:1–5.

The Jewish revolt against the Romans began in AD 66 as an aggressive backlash against the latest procurator, the greedy Florus, who raided the temple treasures. This provoked a Roman response, which included random crucifixion. The final act prior to all-out war was the refusal of a priest, Eleazar, to make the daily sacrifice for the emperor's welfare. The zealots now took the opportunity to march to Jerusalem, forcing the Roman forces to surrender. Rome was stung, but retaliated with massive force and Titus, the son of the emperor, attacked the city in AD 70.

On August 29, on the anniversary of the destruction of the First Temple by the Babylonians, the city was in Roman hands and destroyed. Jews were slaughtered or enslaved and 700 of them were dragged back to Rome as part of the triumphal procession, which included the temple treasures.

So, sadly and inevitably, the two prophecies that Jesus made over Jerusalem were now fulfilled some 40 years later. The 'Promised Land' was again purged of most of its Jewish population and this exile was to prove far longer than the exile under the Babylonians. Meanwhile the faith that grew from the teachings, death and resurrection of Jesus of Nazareth spread throughout the Roman empire, challenging the dominant Greek culture.

European history for the next few centuries was to be moulded by this faith, while the Jews were to languish in the miseries of exile for 19 centuries.

Chapter 5

Palestine

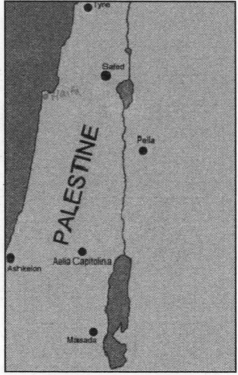

Fig. 6: **Early Palestine**

The name 'Palestine' (or Palastina) was given to the land in AD 135 for one reason and one reason only. It was part of a campaign to strip away any association of the land with the Jewish people. By inventing a name derived from one of the Jews' bitterest ancient enemies, the Philistines, the Romans succeeded in needling Jewish people right up to the current day. It was as if England was renamed Lesser France on account of the French invasion in 1066. Or the USA being referred to as Navajoland in memory of the Native American tribe. It rankled and it was designed to rankle.

How had it come to this? Well, read on . . .

Jerusalem had never seen such misery in the thousand years or so since David made it his capital. It was AD 70 and the Romans had brutalised the city and its inhabitants with an army three times the size of that needed to invade Britain years earlier, killing 600,000 Jews in the aftermath. Referring to this in 1868, CH Spurgeon said *'The destruction of Jerusalem was more terrible than anything that the world has ever witnessed, either before or since.'*[1] The temple had been utterly destroyed and so, almost, had Judaism itself. A leading Pharisee, Yochanan Ben Zakkai, just managed to escape in a coffin and set up an academy in Yavneh by the coast. This subsequently became the centre for the Jewish community in the land and ensured the future of Rabbinic Judaism, the new form of Judaism adapted to function without the temple sacrifices.

Jews who were followers of the new Christian faith had already fled Jerusalem for Pella, to the east of the river Jordan, in response to the prophecy of Jesus in Luke 21:20: *'When you see Jerusalem being surrounded by armies, you will know that its desolation is near.'* After filling in the details of what was to happen with unerring accuracy, Jesus uttered the following pronouncement, recorded in verse 24: *'Jerusalem will be trampled on by the Gentiles until the times of the Gentiles are fulfilled.'* Trample they did – for nearly 1,900 years. God's covenant land was now to be trampled by nations *outside* the covenant He made with Abraham. Let us remind ourselves: this covenant may have promised the land as an eternal possession to the Jewish people, but it doesn't give a timetable of events. For reasons to be discussed later, the Jews now entered an exile, the *Diaspora*, that was to last for nearly 1,900 years.

The story wasn't quite over for the Jews in the land, but it was the beginning of the end of their majority status. Some zealots had a famous last stand at Masada in AD 73, preferring suicide to capture by the Romans and serving as an enduring national symbol of defiance for subsequent generations. Others escaped the enemy's clutches and were sufficiently emboldened to organise a second Jewish revolt. They were led by Simon bar Kochba, who was proclaimed Messiah by a leading scholar, Rabbi Akiva, in order to attach an apocryphal significance to the struggle. Messianic Jews, believing that the Messiah, Jesus, had already come, found it impossible to follow this man, and thus the final split between the Christian Jews and their brethren was cemented.

This revolt exploded in AD 132, significantly on the very same day, the 9th of Av, when both the First and the Second Temples had been destroyed! In order to blot out any Jewish associations with the land, the Romans renamed the city of Jerusalem Aelia Capitolina, forbidding any Jew from living there, and the land was given the name Palestine.

It is interesting to note that in virtually every current Bible you can mention, maps showing Israel in biblical times will invariably have the heading 'Palestine', even though this name was unknown until 100 years after the Resurrection. Scholars are fond of the name Palestine, perhaps not realising that the very use of the word is a provocation to Jewish people. To them it seems to be an affirmation of Arab claims to the land, giving the mistaken impression that the land has always been *Palestinian* land, even going back to biblical times!

As we enter the Times of the Gentiles, we reach a key point in our story. What was happening to the Jews? Were they now cursed by God and, if so, *why*? The early Christians were Jewish, but as more and more Gentiles entered the Church, a time came when Jewish Christians were very much in the minority.

Now we come to the crunch. The Jewish (or Hebraic) worldview that had dominated biblical thought for over 2,000 years now gave way to the dominant worldview of the Gentile world, the Greek philosophies of Aristotle and others. This was to have drastic consequences for the Jewish people.

Many of the early Church Fathers had extensive knowledge of Greek poetry and the writings of the philosophers and, consequently, were heavily influenced by Greek thought patterns. Chief among these was the use of allegory and this led to interpretations of the Bible that were highly symbolic. Origen, in particular, popularised allegorical interpretations of the Bible that have influenced Christian understanding right up to the modern day. This was not good news for the Jewish people.

Once the Church had moved away from its Jewish origins, the Gentile Church Fathers were keen to show the world how the favours of God had moved from the old flesh-and-blood *natural* Israel to the spanking new *spiritual* Israel, the Church. They reasoned that the Jews had had their chance and failed. 'Didn't they bring it on themselves?' they argued. 'For surely they not only rejected Jesus, their Messiah, but they killed him as well!'

It suited them to ignore a few key points:

1. It was the Romans who actually killed Jesus. Crucifixion was a Roman instrument of death.
2. A reading of the Gospels shows that it was the Jewish leadership who bear the responsibility for the rejection of Jesus, not the Jews as a whole. *'But the chief priests and the elders persuaded the crowd to ask for Barabbas and to have Jesus executed'* (Matthew 27:20).
3. Jesus had to die for Christianity to exist. There can be no resurrection without a crucifixion. Is it fair to eternally condemn whoever is responsible for this part in God's plan for mankind?
4. On the cross, Jesus himself forgave the people responsible for his death (Luke 23:34).
5. Jesus knew in advance of his death; he spoke of it earlier to his disciples. It was no surprise to him.

It's a pity that the Church Fathers, of Gentile origin, were unwilling to consider these points. It appears they had their own agenda to follow. These early Christians weren't an ignorant rabble; they were learned men who were zealous in defending their faith, often to the death. Yet they were blinkered when it came to 'the Jewish question'. Why was this? There were four reasons.

Firstly, there was a split between Judaism and early Christianity. The key event was the revolt in AD 132, when the Christians refused to support the Jews and instead fled from Jerusalem. This resulted in great antagonism towards the Christians from the Jews, who at that time were still in the majority.

Secondly, the Christians saw the destruction of Jerusalem as proof that God had turned His back on the Jews and saw themselves as God's new 'chosen people'.

Thirdly, Jews as a whole refused to accept Jesus as Messiah. As a result, some early Christians began to see Jews less as potential converts and more as enemies of the Gospel.

Fourthly, the Church was becoming overwhelmingly Gentile and so the new leaders began to formulate a new theology that accounted for this.

Their conclusions can be summarised thus: God had permanently cut the nation of Israel off as His people as a result of her disobedience and idolatry in the Old Testament, and her rejection and crucifixion of Jesus in the New. The faithful of the Church age became the 'new Israel' of God. The Church would now inherit the promises given to national Israel.

In AD 160 Justin Martyr, living in Asia Minor, wrote a piece called *Dialogue with the Jew Trypho* in which he declared that the (Gentile) Church had completely and permanently replaced Israel in the working out of God's plans and would now inherit all the promises made to Israel in the Old Testament.[2]

The new theology they created to justify these views has become known as *Replacement Theology* and has been a dominant view of the Christian Church ever since. As mentioned earlier, this theology was the product of minds educated in the pagan Greek worldview, a system where the material world was seen as carnal and evil and the spiritual world as the only thing worth striving for.

There are two major elements to Replacement Theology:

1. Rejection of a literal reading of certain biblical scriptures (particularly the Old Testament) and their obvious meanings in order to justify its own positions.
2. The spiritualising of certain biblical scriptures (particularly the Old Testament), using such methods as allegory and functional hermeneutics.

This was great. By extensive use of allegory and symbolism, anyone can make the Bible say anything at all! You can squeeze all sorts of 'new revelations' out of scripture, for example:

- Virtually every person and event in the Old Testament foreshadowed the life and work of Jesus (Justin Martyr).
- Jesus bound Satan at the cross and restrained him from seducing the nations (Augustine).
- The existence of the soul before the body, universal salvation and a 'limited' hell (Origen).

If the Church is the 'new Israel', do the references to Israel in the New Testament obviously refer to the Church? Let's look at the Bible. Of the 77 times the words Israel or Israelite occur in the New Testament:

- In nine cases they are direct quotations from the Old Testament, so the meaning must be the same, e.g. Matthew 2:6: *'But you, Bethlehem, in the land of Judah, are by no means least among the rulers of Judah; for out of you will come a ruler who will be the shepherd of my people Israel'* (quoting Micah 5:2).

- In 66 cases they are not Old Testament quotes but clearly refer to Israel rather than the Church, e.g. Matthew 10:6: '*Go rather to the lost sheep of Israel*', Romans 11:26: '*And so all Israel will be saved*'. Use a concordance or Bible software, see the list for yourself, and be convinced.
- In only two cases (Romans 9:6–9 and Galatians 6:15–16) would this interpretation seem to be an obvious choice, but in both cases, Paul is restricting the use of the word *Israel* to those Jews who had accepted Jesus.

So where did the idea of the Church being the 'new Israel' come from? It certainly doesn't seem to be from a systematic review of the New Testament. The key word is *tradition*. Just as Jesus constantly argued with the Pharisees over their use of the 'traditions of the elders' rather than the Word of God, so we must take his example and do the same, unless we want to follow *Churchianity* rather than Christianity, *tradition* rather than scripture.

In Acts 1:6, when Jesus was asked '*Lord, are you at this time going to restore the kingdom to Israel?*' it would have been a good opportunity for him to answer 'What exactly do you mean by 'Israel' because, you see, I've changed the rules.' But he didn't, because for Jesus, Israel was Israel was *Israel*.

Also, one of the claims of these people is that the Church inherits the blessings promised to Israel in the Old Testament. But what of the curses in the Old Testament? No, we don't want those, we'll leave those with the Jews! Examples of this can be seen by looking at the King James Version of the Bible.

The chapter heading in this Bible above Isaiah 59 reads '*The sins of the Jews*' and the next chapter has the heading '*Glory of the Church*'. Everything that is nice and positive is thus promised to the Church and all the curses are left for the Jews! None of this was in the original biblical text: it was added by English translators who had already made up their minds and wanted to tell the world what they thought.

Needless to say, Mr Shoots has most assuredly bought into this Replacement Theology in one way or another.

Returning to history, we can trace how Replacement Theology became Christian practice. Although the Jews were by then largely living in exile, they were a constant embarrassment to the Church Fathers, who were eager to show the triumph of Christianity over Judaism and Christian over Jew. And what better way to do this than to directly attack the very heart of Judaism, the religious practices.

The day of rest and worship changed to Sunday, the Lord's Day, in honour of Jesus' resurrection. Despite the fact that there was no direction from God on this and that Sunday was a pagan Roman day of sun worship, it was the first step away from the roots and towards the pagan community in which they lived. This, with the later adoption of December 25 as Christmas Day (the Roman day of Saturnalia, a day of orgy and revelry) and of Easter (a pagan fertility festival), went totally against the teaching of Jesus, who told them to '*be in the world, but not of the world*'.

Then it started to get personal.

In the fourth century AD there lived John, called Chrysostom, literally 'the golden-mouthed', by his friends and followers on account of his eloquence in promoting modest Christian principles. He was probably the best-known preacher of the day. What did he think of the Jews? Here are his words:

'The synagogue is not only a whorehouse and a theatre; it is also a den of thieves and a haunt of wild animals . . . not the cave of a wild animal merely, but of an unclean wild animal . . . The Jews have no conception of things at all, but living for the lower nature, all agog for the here and now, no better disposed than pigs or goats, they live by the rule of debauchery and inordinate gluttony. Only one thing they understand: to gorge themselves and get drunk.'[3]

Can you believe these words? Chrysostom wasn't alone in expressing these sentiments; it's just that his writings have survived longer than those of his contemporaries. You can imagine a small rabble meeting in a darkened room in a sordid part of town and spewing out such views out of ignorance and hatred, but coming from the mouth of the 'greatest of Christian preachers', who was renowned for his moral teaching, it is unbelievable! We are now entering a situation that becomes very difficult to understand from a natural standpoint. It would be understandable for this Christian leader to preach his views on the 'rejection of the Jews', but then, out of common humanity, also to urge forgiveness and understanding. After all, this is what Jesus taught!

Chrysostom continues: *'As for me, I hate the synagogue . . . I hate the Jews . . .'*

Now you may think that I have been uncharitable to Chrysostom, because after all we only picked on some of his writings, ignoring the rest of his life's work. Perhaps we can allow him one little lapse; he may have been having a 'bad hair day' when he wrote those horrible things. No, certainly not! We can only judge historical figures by the effect they have on the world, and the anti-Semitic writings of Chrysostom, along with many other Church fathers such as Augustine, Tertullian, Origen, Irenaeus and others, set the tone for treatment of the Jews in subsequent years.

Most of this chapter has been a deviation from the straight historical narrative of previous chapters and, for some of you, this has probably been a hard slog. But I make no excuses, because it is important for us to gain an understanding of the teaching and the practical action that they inspired.

While we're on the subject of theology, let's consider another difficult question. Why were the Jews exiled from the land under the Romans anyway? Did God reject the Jews, as Replacement Theology says? Let's just look at some scriptures and, in true Hebraic style, read them in a plain, literal sense. I will let the scriptures speak for themselves.

> *'But you, O Israel, my servant, Jacob, whom I have chosen, you descendants of Abraham my friend, I took you from the ends of the earth, from its farthest corners I called you. I said, "You are my servant"; I have chosen you and have not rejected you'* (Isaiah 41:8–9).

> *'This is what the Lord says, he who appoints the sun to shine by day, who decrees the moon and stars to shine by night, who stirs up the sea so that its waves roar – the Lord Almighty is his name: "Only if these decrees vanish from my sight," declares the Lord, "will the descendants of Israel ever cease to be a nation before me"'* (Jeremiah 31:35–36).

> *'How can I give you up, Ephraim? How can I hand you over, Israel? . . . For I am God, and not man'* (Hosea 11:8–9).

> *'I have loved you with an everlasting love'* (Jeremiah 31:3).

'O descendants of Israel his servant, O sons of Jacob, his cho-sen ones. He is the Lord our God; his judgments are in all the earth. He remembers his covenant for ever, the word he com-manded, for a thousand generations, the covenant he made with Abraham, the oath he swore to Isaac. He confirmed it to Jacob as a decree, to Israel as an everlasting covenant' (1Chronicles 16:13–17).

'For the Lord's portion is his people, Jacob his allotted inheri-tance' (Deuteronomy 32:9).

'He has revealed his word to Jacob, his laws and decrees to Israel. He has done this for no other nation' (Psalm 147:19–20).

'The Lord will not reject his people; he will never forsake his inheritance' (Psalm 94:14).

'Remember that at that time you were separate from Christ, excluded from citizenship in Israel and foreigners to the covenants of the promise . . . Consequently, you are no longer foreigners and aliens, but fellow-citizens with God's people and members of God's household' (Ephesians 2:12,19).

'The law, introduced 430 years later, does not set aside the covenant previously established by God and thus do away with the promise. For if the inheritance depends on the law, then it no longer depends on a promise; but God in his grace gave it to Abraham through a promise' (Galatians 3:17–18).

'9–11' has entered public consciousness as a watershed event in the modern world, when the old certainties crumbled as dramatically as the Twin Towers. Yet there's another '9–11', mostly ignored by the Church since Bible translators arbitrarily divided up Paul's letters to the Christian communities of his day. Romans '9–11', the 'missing chapters' that bridge the supposed gap between 'nothing separating us from the love of God' and 'offering our bodies as living sacrifices', is as neglected by pulpit preachers as Isaiah 53 ('the suffering servant') is by the Jewish rabbis in orthodox synagogues. It is embarrassing; it doesn't fit in. It talks of things that simply don't square with the carefully constructed arguments of Mr Shoots. It speaks of the Jews . . . having a future!

As Paul asserts in Romans 11:1, *'I ask then: Did God reject his people? By no means!'* God may be punishing the Jewish people during the exile, or Diaspora, according to the terms of the covenant with Moses, but He *hasn't* abandoned them.

And God provides a stark warning to the Gentile Church. The Jews, natural Israel, are considered the natural branches of a spiritual olive tree. Gentiles are to be considered wild, grafted-in branches.

> *'Do not be arrogant, but be afraid. For if God did not spare the natural branches, he will not spare you either'* (Romans 11:20–21).

Be afraid!

Did they heed this warning? Let's return to our historical narrative and find out.

After the second Jewish revolt, the centre of Judaism moved to the north, to Galilee, which held the largest concentration of Jews in the country. Gentiles were concentrated on the coastal plain. The next event of historical note was the Christianisation of Europe under Emperor Constantine in the fourth century and the official beginning of state-sponsored anti-Semitism, on the pretext that the Church had supplanted the Jewish people as 'God's chosen' and therefore the Jews 'must be utterly rejected by God', giving the Church the right to 'carry out God's will' in persecuting Jews at every opportunity.

Christianity returned to Palestine with a vengeance under the banner of the Byzantine empire. In AD 326, Constantine built the Church of the Holy Sepulchre in Jerusalem on the supposed site of Jesus' burial and the city became the spiritual capital of the empire. Missionary work commenced in Galilee, provoking a Jewish revolt in AD 351 and, although this area continued to be an important Jewish centre, many churches were built there alongside the synagogues. There were also troubles between Jews and Christians in Samaria. The revolt, already mentioned, led to the destruction of many Jewish settlements there.

The coastal cities, such as Gaza and Ashkelon, with a lower Jewish population, became important commercial centres, exporting, among other things, religious para-phernalia – after all, this was a Holy Land – to the rest of the Christian world. The southern area of the land, the Negev, became a favourite among the new Christian inhabitants. The deep south was used as a place of exile for misbehaving bishops and the Sinai area was already attracting the interest of pilgrims and religious tourists.

In AD 614 the Persian empire came to visit, conquering Jerusalem in the usual brutal manner of despotic empires, burning many of the churches that had sprung up there and killing many priests. For the only time in history there were no Jewish deaths – Jews, if you remember, had largely been expelled from the city by the Romans 500 years earlier.

As Christianity, through Emperor Constantine, had become the state religion, there was now a good living to be made as professional Christians. Overnight the common man found out that whereas yesterday he had been a pagan, indulging in vile practices and worshipping a selection of gods, today he was officially 'Christian', whatever that meant, now worshipping only one God (and his mother, Mary). It didn't stop the vile practices, however, and as no-one was given a Bible to read (that was a privilege left to the clergy), they had no idea what was acceptable behaviour. Mind you, no-one seemed to mind how you treated the Jews; in fact, the clergy positively encouraged nasty behaviour towards this 'accursed' people.

The 'official version' of Christianity, however, was at that time by and large a trillion miles away from anything described in the New Testament, and God showed what He thought about this state of affairs by allowing them to sink into the Dark Ages, a period of intellectual and spiritual darkness in the 'civilized world' lasting for centuries. And as a further punishment, there was a stirring in the Arabian desert . . .

NOTES

[1] Charles Spurgeon, *Commentary on Matthew* (1868), p. 412.
[2] Justin Martyr, *Dialogue with the Jew Trypho*, Chapter 135.
[3] John Chrysostom, *Eight Orations Against the Jews*, pp. 1,3,4.

Chapter 6

The Holy Land

(AD614)

At about that time came the event that is very much at the heart of the current conflict. A 40-year-old Arab called Muhammad had a religious experience and Islam was born.

In order to get a grasp of current claims on the land by Muslims, it is important that we go back to the beginning, to Muhammad himself, to see what he had to say about the Jews, the land and Jerusalem.

Muhammad's relationship with the Jews follows a theme that is all too familiar, particularly when we look at the attitudes of Christian leaders such as Martin Luther. It starts off with respect for a people who have stubbornly and faithfully clung to their God despite all the world had to throw at them. It continues with attempts to convert these people to your way of thinking and ends, unsurprisingly, with frustrated anger, leading to persecution, when they don't dance to your tune.

Muhammad and his followers stayed for ten years in Medina, a place with a thriving Jewish population. One of the first things he did there was strike a covenant with the Jewish inhabitants, promising good relations. He then set out to win them over, as is indicated by a verse in the Qur'an, his holy book: '*We gave the Book to the*

Israelites and bestowed on them wisdom and prophethood. We provided them with wholesome things and exalted them above the nation. [1] Muhammad was an Ishmaelite, meaning that he shared a common ancestor with the Jews – Ishmael was Abraham's first-born son, by the slave girl Hagar. He played on this, trying to gain converts among the Jews, but ultimately failed to win them over. Because of this, he broke away from them in AD 624 and started to strip away some Jewish elements from his new religion. The direction of prayer was moved from Jerusalem to Mecca (its original direction before his move to Medina). He broke his covenant with them, justifying his actions in the Qur'an: *'If you fear treachery from any of your allies, you may fairly retaliate by breaking off your treaty with them. God does not love the treacherous.'* [2] As his influence grew in Medina, there followed a period of persecutions, assassinations and expulsions of the Jews.

Muslims identify Jerusalem as the third holiest site of the Islamic faith. We must ask ourselves why that should be, as the name *Jerusalem* does not appear once in the Qur'an (though it appears over 700 times in the Old Testament), neither does it appear in Muslim prayers. The only justification given is the claim that Muhammad himself visited Jerusalem in a dream and from there 'ascended to heaven'. The Qur'an states *'Glory be to Him who made His servant go by night from the Sacred Temple to the farther Temple whose surroundings we have blessed, that We might show him some of Our signs. He alone hears all and observes all.'* [3]

The *Sacred Temple* refers to Mecca and the *farther Temple*, supposedly, to Jerusalem. There is confusion regarding this farther temple, as at that time there was no temple, Jewish or Muslim, of any kind in Jerusalem! Some commentators have even said that this farther temple was a mosque elsewhere in Arabia. Others have said that the farther temple is the al-Aqsa Mosque that can still be seen today in the Old City of Jerusalem. The only problem is that this mosque was built in the reign of Umar, at some time after AD 635, but Muhammad had died three years earlier.

A few years after Muhammad's death, the Muslims were in the land, having defeated the Romans at the battle of Yarmouk. They captured Jerusalem from the Byzantines, who had wrenched it back from the Persians nine years earlier. On the Temple mount they built the shrine of the Dome of the Rock in AD 691, still there today as the city's most recognisable and controversial feature. The land was now generally named the *Holy Land* by the Christian world.

Yet it was welcome relief from Byzantine rule as Jews were now allowed back into Jerusalem and, in general, Jewish communities throughout the land were allowed to prosper, particularly in Tiberias in Galilee. Under Muslim rule, Jews were considered as one of the 'peoples of the Book' and were given a protected status, a much better deal than state Christianity ever gave them! The Muslims used the coastal cities of Tyre, Acre and Caesarea pretty much as their Christian predecessors had, as important centres of commerce with the outside world. Later on in their rule they even populated these towns with Muslims from other parts of their empire, such as Persia, in order to strengthen their hold. These tended to be soldiers, to fight off constant attack from Byzantine ships from the west. The Negev, of earlier interest for Christian pilgrims, was now a place of interest for Muslim pilgrims, as it was an important route to Islamic holy places.

At this time, Jerusalem had little importance in the Muslim world. The first description of the town under

Muslim rule comes from the visiting Bishop Arculf, a Gallic pilgrim, in AD 680, who reported seeing *'an oblong house of prayer, which they [the Muslims] pieced together with upright planks and large beams over some ruined remains.'*[4] At no time had Jerusalem ever been a capital city in the Muslim world. In fact, the only times Jerusalem has ever been clothed with importance and significance in the Muslim world it has been as a response to external events, such as the Crusades and the Jewish regathering (both to be discussed later).

From AD 750, Jerusalem fell into near-obscurity. For the next three-and-a-half centuries, Muslim books praising this city lost favour, no more glorious buildings were built and the city walls collapsed. The city declined to the point of becoming a shambles. *'Learned men are few, and the Christians numerous,'* cried a tenth-century Muslim native of Jerusalem.[5] The great historian SD Goitein concludes that, in its first six centuries of Muslim rule, *'Jerusalem mostly lived the life of an out-of-the-way provincial town, delivered to the exactions of rapacious officials and notables, often also to tribulations at the hands of seditious fellahin [peasants] or nomads . . . Jerusalem certainly could not boast of excellence in the sciences of Islam or any other fields.'*[6]

Muslim rule in the land had its first major test at the hands of the Crusaders, in what has been described as 'one of the most romantic, chaotic, cruel, passionate, bizarre and dramatic episodes in history'. This was the eleventh century AD and various ill-advised armies of 'Christians' from Europe were led by soldiers and priests to the Holy Land, under the Pope's instruction.

They came to reclaim 'Christian land' from the 'infidel Muslims', which was a quite ridiculous idea as there is no such thing as 'Christian land'. Of course, scripture states most clearly that the Holy Land is God's land, with Jews as the rightful tenants according to the covenant with Abraham. But nowhere is it ever called 'Christian land'. This mob of 'pilgrims' inflamed by disease, hunger and religious fanaticism killed all in their path, including other Christians in the lands to the east, whom they mistook for 'infidels'.

The initial Muslim response to the First Crusade was minimal, but it all changed when Jerusalem was threatened. In order to drum up support in the Muslim world, the status of this neglected outpost was drastically heightened. Through books, poems and sacred literature, propaganda was produced stressing the sanctity of Jerusalem and the urgency of its return to Muslim rule. Suddenly Jerusalem became ever more critical to the Islamic faith, a situation unheard of just a few years earlier!

The First Crusade (1096–1099) was the most successful. Let us look at the sequence of events leading to this infamous episode.

About 50 years earlier, Turks had invaded the region, converted to Islam and subdued the reigning Arab power. These new invaders were even more aggressive toward the Christians than their predecessors, meaning that pilgrimage routes, long protected by the Byzantines and friendly Arab rulers, were closed down and Christians could no longer walk where Jesus had walked.

The Byzantine emperor appealed to the West for help and in 1095, Pope Urban II responded, in a speech delivered at Clermont in central France. He called for a crusade to save the Christian East from Islam. The Turks, Urban reportedly said, were *'disembowelling Christians and dumping the bloody viscera on church altars and baptismal fonts'*. Those who joined this crusade would have their sins absolved, for God Himself desired that Christianity should recover Jerusalem.

On July 15, 1099, after a two-week siege of Jerusalem, the Crusaders broke through. The city's Muslim rulers surrendered without a fight and, in the three days of celebrations, the conquerors slaughtered nearly every Muslim in the city and burned down a synagogue in which Jews had sought refuge. Contemporary accounts spoke of the blood that flooded the city to the height of the horses' knees. Having conquered the land, the Crusader leaders started taking steps to possess it. Over the next few years they secured the coastal cities of Caesarea, Haifa and Acre. Baldwin was proclaimed the first king of the 'Latin Kingdom of Jerusalem' and his successors built a series of fortresses from the Dead Sea to the Gulf of Aqaba. They also captured Ashkelon from the Egyptian Fatimids, who were using the city's port to conduct raids against the Crusader kingdom.

By the mid-twelfth century, the Latin Kingdom of Jerusalem controlled the territories of present-day Israel, western Jordan and southern Lebanon. In Jerusalem itself, the Dome of the Rock was converted into a church, the Templum Domini, with architectural changes inside and outside. The al-Aqsa Mosque, by the Temple mount, was used as a residence, first for the Crusader kings and then for the Knights Templar, a holy order later to become an elite fighting force. But this rule wasn't to last long. The sultan Saladin, who unified Egypt and Syria, attacked the Crusader kingdom from the north in 1187, defeating the army of the Latin Kingdom of Jerusalem at the Horns of Hattin, west of the Sea of Galilee, and took control of Jerusalem and the whole country.

Crusader rule in Jerusalem had lasted a mere 90 years. This pleased the Crusaders not at all and they made a comeback in 1189 in the Third Crusade under Richard the Lionheart, but never managed to extend further than the coastal regions, a thin strip along the Mediterranean. Richard signed a treaty with Saladin, which at least granted rights for pilgrims to visit Jerusalem. The city was finally retaken 40 years later through the Sixth Crusade, resulting in 15 years of Crusader rule. This was ended by an invasion of Mongols from Central Asia, who wreaked havoc in the city, destroying many of the Crusader buildings.

In the late thirteenth century, a new force arose in Egypt: the Mamluks, fierce warriors who invaded the Holy Land, evicting the Mongols and regaining Crusader possessions. The last Crusader outpost, the city of Acre, fell in 1291, putting an end to the European presence in the land. The Mamluks began destroying every Crusader site that fell into their hands and managed to sustain a state that lasted for over 300 years, until 1560. They destroyed all the fortifications along the coast and much of the population moved to the mountain regions. The coastal plain remained desolate for centuries afterwards, with vegetation growing wild and swampland a dominant feature.

Jerusalem was generally ignored and used as a place of exile for out-of-favour officials. These people started a building programme and the city began to take on a Muslim appearance although, at this time, the city was unwalled and vulnerable to attack. In fact, it was attacked in 1219 and not rebuilt for three centuries. By the end of Mamluk rule there were barely 4,000 people living in Jerusalem. It was just as well that this was one of the more peaceful periods of its history. Yet during these uncertain times, the Jews still maintained a foothold in the land, particularly in Galilee. The town of

Safed became, by the fifteenth century, the largest Jewish settlement in the whole country.

In 1517, yet another Gentile power came visiting: this time it was the turn of the Ottoman Turks. Although the heads of the Jewish community in Safed were massacred, this didn't lead to a widespread bloodbath and the occupation was generally a peaceful one. It started well for Jerusalem, with the city walls being rebuilt in 1537, but things went slowly downhill from then onwards. The key administrative centres were Nablus and Gaza, and Jerusalem was left to stagnate. Reports from pilgrims, diplomats and tourists bore evidence to this. George Sandys in 1611 found that *'much lies waste; the old buildings (except a few) all ruined, the new contemptible'*. Constantin Volney, one of the most scientific of observers, noted in 1784 Jerusalem's *'destroyed walls, its debris-filled moat, its city circuit choked with ruins'*. *'Hapless are the favourites of heaven,'* commented Herman Melville in 1857.

The first couple of centuries of Ottoman rule were reasonably benevolent, but by the seventeenth century, corruption had set in, with rulers often living vast distances from their regions of control. Local rulers rose up against the central government and created independent states for themselves, only to be ousted by the government. There were many such conflicts, too many to outline here. The effect of all of this misrule was that the land fell into ruin. Yet during this time Safed's reputation grew, with Jews flocking there from Spain and Portugal. The town in time became a centre for mysticism, specifically Kabbalism. Jerusalem was of little importance for the Turks, as for their predecessors, though the walls were rebuilt and the Dome of the Rock renovated.

The Ottoman empire began to crumble in the nineteenth century, with a rise in the influence of European powers. In the 1840s, there was an immigration of the Druze from Lebanon in the north, as a result of French meddling. There was also an immigration of Muslims from Bulgaria and Sudan into the Golan, to the north. Many other Arab workers were to migrate to the Holy Land later in the nineteenth century. There was a lot of European influence in the affairs of Jerusalem, responsible for new religious and government buildings. Protestant Christians also began arriving in increasing numbers. The Ottomans welcomed them all, as it all meant extra taxes from them.

Alongside this steady influx, another group of people were beginning to return to the land of their forefathers and, more importantly, the land of their covenant with God. These were the Jews. Although they had always had a presence there over the previous 17 centuries, their main concentration had been outside the land, in exile, or diaspora. But there were now stirrings in the air and it seemed that the days were numbered for the 'times of the Gentiles'.

NOTES

1 Qur'an 45:16.
2 Qur'an 8:58.
3 Qur'an 17:1.
4 FE Peters, *Jerusalem*, pp. 195–196.
5 Guy Le Strange, *Palestine Under the Moslems* (Boston, Houghton Mifflin, 1890), p. 86.
6 SD Goitein, 'Al-Kuds', *The Encyclopaedia of Islam*, 2nd edn, vol. 5, pp. 329, 322.

Chapter 7

Zion

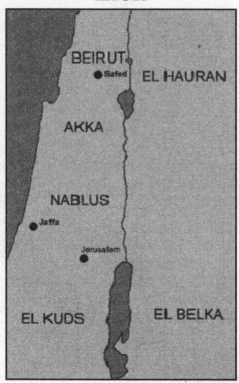

Fig. 7: **Palestine under Turkish rule**

In 1816, a comfortable English family produced a baby boy. Young John grew up to be a keen sportsman with a lively intelligence and was destined for the family business. It all went wrong when the family business collapsed and, as a last resort, John was ordained into the Church. He eventually became the first Bishop of Liverpool, but it was his writings that cemented his place in history. Because, you see, JC Ryle was a Christian writer of rare clarity and prophetic insight. It was said that he 'changed the face of the English Church'. Of interest to us, he published a sermon entitled 'Scattered Israel to be gathered'[1] at a time when the Jews were indeed scattered to the ends of the Earth, a despised and unloved people, stateless and without real hope . . . or so it seemed.

The text of his sermon was Jeremiah 31:10: '*Hear the word of the Lord, O nations; proclaim it in distant coastlands: He who scattered Israel will gather them and will watch over his flock like a shepherd.*'

He then wrote on four points. Firstly, in the light of the Replacement Theology that had become the norm in the Church, he defined his understanding of the word 'Israel' as being '*the whole Jewish nation*' and urged his listeners to '*cleave to the literal sense of Bible words, and beware of departing from it, except in cases of absolute necessity. Beware of that system of allegorising and spiritualising, and accommodating, which the school of Origen first brought in, and which has found such an unfortunate degree of favour in the Church*'.

The second point he made concerned the '*present condition of Israel*', which, of course, was the situation in the mid-nineteenth century, a full century before Israel was to become a recognised nation. He noted that '*scattered as they are, there is a national vitality among them which is stronger than that of any nation on earth*'.

He then addressed the vital question that cuts to the very heart of the matter and that is the most troubling

issue of all. Why so painful, why so long? The exile to
Babylon only lasted 70 years or so, but this one had lasted
for 1,800 years and there was no sign of an end to it. Why,
why, why? JC Ryle was very clear in his understanding. It
was a result of their many sins. *'Their hardness and stiff-*
neckedness, their impenitence and unbelief, their abuse of
privileges and neglect of gifts, their rejection of prophets and
messengers from heaven, and finally their refusal to receive the
Lord Jesus Christ, the King's own Son, these were the things
which called down God's wrath upon them.'

This is heavy stuff, highly politically incorrect by
today's standards. He used the Jewish people as an
object lesson to the Gentile Church, a warning against
spiritual pride and self-righteousness and the exaltation
of men's traditions over the Word of God. He warns the
Church against its own complacency in these matters.
'Let us each look to ourselves and take heed to our own souls.
The same God lives who scattered Israel because of Israel's
sins. And what says He to the Churches of Christ this day? He
says, "Be not high-minded, but fear. If God spared not the nat-
ural branches, take heed lest He also spares not thee" (Romans
11:20–21).'

This is a strong lesson and a hard one, particularly
when one considers the consequences of this divine policy. After all, the horrors of the Holocaust were arguably
the natural outcome of centuries of 'Christian
anti-Semitism', Hitler even using as justification of his
anti-Jewish rantings the writings of Martin Luther, the
chief architect of the Reformation.

The problem of the Gentile Church over these centuries is adequately summarised by a neat saying from
the mouth of Jesus himself: *'Why do you look at the speck of*
sawdust in your brother's eye and pay no attention to the
plank in your own eye?' (Matthew 7:3).

The sins of the Jewish people leading to their exile were played out in our full view, because, after all, wasn't this one of the main themes of the Bible? We read of God's faithfulness to His chosen people, repaid by their rejection of His prophets and their Messiah. We use these episodes as teaching points, but we can easily forget that these important lessons have been bought at a heavy price for the Jewish people, in biblical times and thereafter. We read of the sins of David, of Solomon, of the kings of Israel and Judah, of the scribes and Pharisees, and we are quick to judge them, we are ready to criticise them by saying 'How could they repay God in this way for all He did for them? He gave them manna in the desert, He gave them victory in battle, He gave them healing and salvation through the ministry of Jesus. How could they turn their back on Him? No wonder He turned His back on them!' It is easy for us, from the comfort of our armchairs, to make these accusations, isn't it? Yet, consider this . . .

The interactions of God with humanity can also be seen in the pages of history, a *third* testament, as it were, to be considered alongside the Old Testament and the New Testament. We'll call it the 'Last Testament'. He wasn't going to add in any more covenants; after all, the ministry of Jesus was the final word as far as salvation is concerned and the covenant with Abraham was pretty watertight too. No, the purpose of the Last Testament is simply to be a record of the historical Church from the time of the Church Fathers to the present. The books of this Last Testament would be a series of letters (or e-mails?) by a modern-day 'Paul' to the Church at large.

There would be much that was good, life affirming and heartening. But there would also be some dark chapters, reminiscent of the gloomier sections of the Old

Testament prophets. Book titles could be 'concerning the Crusades', 'concerning the Inquisition', 'concerning Church traditions', 'concerning Holy War', but the main thrust would be a modern day 'Romans': perhaps we'll call it 'Jerusalem'. This would be a letter specifically written to Jewish Christian fellowships in Jerusalem and would be a list of all the sins committed by an unforgiving and self-righteous Gentile Church against the Jewish people over the centuries, ranging from insults and accusations to deportation, murder and massacre. It would mention the fact that all these actions were committed by 'Christians' working from a fundamentally flawed understanding of the mind of God, carrying out judgements on behalf of God on a people it considered cursed.

Now the point of all this is that the sins that so called 'Christians' over the centuries have committed are at a level far exceeding anything the Jews did. Yet the Jews received a 1,900-year exile for their misdemeanours! What does the 'Gentile Church' deserve? You may point out the fact that the Jews were ultimately exiled (and 'rejected') for their rejection of Jesus their Messiah, but is that any worse than the indescribably evil acts committed by 'Christians' *in the name of Jesus*? The Jews rejected salvation through their Messiah, but were the hymn-singing 'Christian' Crusaders who waded through the blood of slaughtered Jews and Muslims in Jerusalem truly following the words of Jesus?

Let's imagine that the Gentile Church received the same punishment as the Jews of old and we're now in the twenty-fifth century looking back, reading the Last Testament, noticing that the descendants of those Gentile Christians are themselves wandering the world without a home. Would we read about their sins and call them an accursed people too? *'Do not judge or you too will be judged. For in the same way as you judge others, you will be judged, and with the measure you use, it will be measured to you'* (Matthew 7:1–2). So the lesson we should take from this is that God alone is our judge and *only* God is in a position to judge others, whether Christian, unbeliever, Jew or Gentile.

3. Returning to JC Ryle, his third point concerned *'the future prospects of Israel'*. This is interesting because what was still very much in the future for this nineteenth century writer is now largely in the present. In fact, he admitted that he was moving into the area of 'unfulfilled prophecy'. He was utterly convinced of the restoration of the Jewish people to their land and mentions that *'out of the sixteen prophets of the Old Testament, there are at least ten in which the gathering and restoration of the Jews in the latter days are expressly mentioned'*.

He then chooses a single scripture from each of these ten prophets, allowing them to speak for themselves. I have taken the liberty of emphasising the key points in bold.

1. *'In that day the Lord will reach out his hand **a second time** to reclaim the remnant that is left of his people from Assyria, from Lower Egypt, from Upper Egypt, from Cush, from Elam, from Babylonia, from Hamath and from the islands of the sea. He will raise a banner for the nations and gather the exiles of Israel; he will **assemble the scattered people of Judah from the four quarters of the earth'*** (Isaiah 11:11–12).

2. *'This is what the Sovereign Lord says: I will take the Israelites out of the nations where they have gone. I will gather them from all around and **bring them back into their own land'*** (Ezekiel 37:21).

3. '*The people of Judah and the people of Israel will be reunited,
and they will appoint one leader and will come up out of
the land, for great will be the day of Jezreel . . . For the Israelites
will live for many days without king or prince, without
sacrifice or sacred stones, without ephod or idol. Afterwards
the Israelites will return and seek the Lord their God and
David their king. They will come trembling to the Lord and to
his blessings in the last days'* (Hosea 1:11; 3:4–5).

4. '*Judah will be inhabited for ever and Jerusalem through all
generations'* (Joel 3:20).

5. '*"I will bring back my exiled people Israel; they will rebuild the
ruined cities and live in them. They will plant vineyards and
drink their wine; they will make gardens and eat their fruit. I
will plant Israel in their own land, never again to be
uprooted from the land I have given them," says the Lord
your God'* (Amos 9:14–15).

6. '*But on Mount Zion will be deliverance; it will be holy, and the
house of Jacob will possess its inheritance'* (Obadiah 17).

7. '*"In that day," declares the Lord, "I will gather the lame; I will
assemble the exiles and those I have brought to grief. I will
make the lame a remnant, those driven away a strong nation.
The Lord will rule over them in Mount Zion from that
day and for ever"'* (Micah 4:6–7).

8. '*At that time I will deal with all who oppressed you; I will
rescue the lame and gather those who have been scattered. I
will give them praise and honour in every land where they
were put to shame. At that time I will gather you; at that
time I will bring you home. I will give you honour and
praise among all the peoples of the earth when I restore your*

fortunes before your very eyes," says the Lord' (Zephaniah 3:19–20).

9. *'Though I scatter them among the peoples, yet in distant lands they will remember me. They and their children **will survive, and they will return**. I will bring them back from Egypt and gather them from Assyria. I will bring them to Gilead and Lebanon, and there will not be room enough for them'* (Zechariah 10:9–10).

10. *'"The days are coming," declares the Lord, "when I will bring my people Israel and Judah back from captivity and **restore them to the land I gave to their forefathers to possess,"** says the Lord . . . "I am with you and will save you," declares the Lord. "Though I completely destroy all the nations among which I scatter you, **I will not completely destroy you.** I will discipline you but only with justice; I will not let you go entirely unpunished"'* (Jeremiah 30:3,11).

These are just a very small sample of the vast quantity of verses that speak on this subject. Some have argued that these verses speak of the Jewish return from Babylon, which is very hard to justify in most cases. As has been stressed earlier, I will let the plain and simple meaning of these verses speak for itself and clear away any doubt as to their true significance.

JC Ryle makes an interesting comment regarding this regathering. *'I might show you by scriptural evidence that the Jews will probably first be gathered in an unconverted state, though humbled, and will afterwards be taught to look to Him whom they have pierced, through much tribulation.'*

Remember, this is not the 'prophecy of justification' *after the event*, this is an Anglican Bishop's reading of scripture a full century before the world had started to see the incredible fulfilment of the Word of God.

There is a fourth point to Bishop Ryle's sermon, but I will leave that until later on, when it is more relevant to the discussion.

The idea of a Jewish homeland in Palestine, though present in Jewish hearts since the start of the exile all those centuries earlier, really took hold of Christian minds at the start of the nineteenth century. It all started (probably) with the Frenchman, Napoleon Bonaparte, who promised Palestine to the Jews. The trouble was that he failed to conquer the land, so it wasn't his to give away! Subsequently, particularly in Britain, we see many prominent people – churchmen, writers, artists and statesmen – all of one mind on the Jewish issue: the need for a Jewish homeland. Among these people were Lord Lindsay, Lord Palmerston, Benjamin Disraeli, William Wilberforce, Charles Spurgeon, Lord Manchester, Holman Hunt, George Eliot, Lord Shaftesbury and, of course, Bishop JC Ryle.

Let us remind ourselves of Isaiah 11:11–12, where we read '*In that day the Lord will reach out his hand **a second time** to reclaim the remnant that is left of His people from Assyria, from Lower Egypt, from Upper Egypt, from Cush, from Elam, from Babylonia, from Hamath and from the islands of the sea. He will raise a banner for the nations and gather the exiles of Israel; he will assemble the scattered people of Judah from the four quarters of the earth.*'

The first regathering had been from the Babylonian empire around 2,500 years earlier. This was the second regathering and God's prophetic timetable had kicked in after centuries of silence.

Lord Shaftesbury was the most loved politician and one of the most effective social reformers in nineteenth-century Britain. He became interested in the Jews through his study of biblical prophecy – he was so keen to understand the Old Testament that he forced himself to learn Hebrew for that very purpose. He became convinced that the Jews should be encouraged to return to Palestine, their God-given home, and encouraged Palmerston, the British Foreign Secretary, to do something about it politically. Such was the might of the British empire in those days that it seems the British were free to do what they liked because, as a result of Shaftesbury's prompting, Michael Alexander, a Jewish Christian, was sent to the Holy Land as the first Bishop of Jerusalem in modern times. Although this man only lived for another couple of years, and the scheme only lasted for 50 years, it represented solid achievement in the desire for an eventual Jewish homeland in Palestine.

In the nineteenth century, Palestine was a poor country, ruled by absentee Turkish landlords as part of the crumbling and corrupt Ottoman empire. By all accounts the land was largely barren and uninhabited, its population either nomadic or involved with agriculture, despite the poor environment. Sir John William Dawson, writing in 1888, said *'No national union and no national spirit has prevailed there. The motley impoverished tribes which have occupied it have held it as mere tenants at will, temporary landowners, evidently waiting for those entitled to the permanent possession of the soil.'*[2] In 1835 Alphonse de Lamartine wrote *'Outside the gates of Jerusalem we saw indeed no living object, heard no living sound, we found the same void, the same silence . . .'*[3]

Thanks to the Turks, the land had been totally neglected. Hundreds of years of abuse had turned the country into a treeless waste, with malaria-ridden swamps, a sprinkling of towns and an uninhabitable desert in the south. This was the position in 1880, and this is incontestable fact.

But now we start to get discrepancies. How many people did live in the land at that time, and who were they? Jewish sources put the figure at between 100,000 and 250,000. Arab sources put the figure at about 480,000 (456,000 Arab, 24,000 Jewish). And who were these Arabs? Arab sources would simply say that these were indigenous people, Arabs who had lived in this land for generations. Jewish and independent sources say otherwise. They point to immigrations from Egypt (to escape heavy taxes), Algeria, Turkey and elsewhere. There are suggestions that up to 25 per cent of the Muslim population of Palestine in the nineteenth century were immigrants.

A final word here from the author of 'Tom Sawyer' and 'Huckleberry Finn'. According to the American author Mark Twain's eyewitness account in 1867, 'The Innocents Abroad', the land was barely populated, just a collection of small villages in a dry, barren land. Here's his summary:

'Of all the lands there are for dismal scenery, I think Palestine must be the prince . . . It is a hopeless, dreary, heart-broken land . . . Palestine sits in sackcloth and ashes. Over it broods the spell of a curse that has withered its fields and fettered its energies . . . Nazareth is forlorn; about that ford of Jordan where the hosts of Israel entered the Promised Land with songs of rejoicing, one finds only a squalid camp of fantastic Bedouins of the desert; Jericho the accursed lies a mouldering ruin, to-day, even as Joshua's miracle left it more than three thousand years ago . . . Renowned Jerusalem itself, the stateliest name in history, has lost all its ancient grandeur, and

is become a pauper village . . . Capernaum is a shapeless ruin;
Magdala is the home of beggared Arabs; Bethsaida and
Chorazin have vanished from the earth . . . Palestine is desolate
and unlovely. And why should it be otherwise? Can the curse
of the Deity beautify a land?'[4]

Palestine was simply an outpost of the Ottoman empire,
a part of Greater Syria. It was not a country or a state in
the manner of, say, Britain or France at that time. It was
simply a collection of villages that happen to exist within the geographical region known as Palestine. Although
many Arabs did own their own homes, the majority
were the poor 'fellahin' who worked as hired hands for
the landowners. There was no nationalism in the land,
no feeling of belonging to a 'people'; loyalty was to the
local clan or village. Arabs did not see themselves as
'Palestinians' and often referred to their homeland as
Southern Syria.

Jews had lived in the land from biblical times,
although in the nineteenth century they were very much
the minority. The first major wave of Jewish immigration
started in the 1880s and by the end of the nineteenth century the Jewish population had tripled to over 80,000
(according to Arab sources).

This included the foundation of the Jewish settlement
of Rishon-le-Zion, where 40 Jewish families settled – followed later by more than 400 Arab families from Egypt
and elsewhere. This was a community that worked and
was at peace. The Arabs saw the benefits of what the
Jews were doing to the land and joined them. Between
1882 and 1914 pioneering Jews started gradually to
transform the land. They worked on the swamps and the
undrained rivers. Life was tough: if you didn't die of
malaria, you could be killed by Bedouins. Soon Jewish

villages were springing up all over, and the towns of Jerusalem, Tiberias, Safed and Haifa started to grow. In 1909, they founded the first modern Jewish city, Tel Aviv. Life was still tough, although disease wasn't so much the problem. Attacks by Arab neighbours increased, even though, through the efforts of these Jewish pioneers, life for all in the land was improving – including for the Arab neighbours.

The motivation for this new zeal for the land was the secular and political movement called Zionism, a desire to return to Zion, their name for this historic homeland of the Jewish people. This shows us that God doesn't just use believers to achieve His ends. He could also use Theodore Herzl, a Jewish atheist working as a journalist in France. Appalled at the anti-Semitism that he observed as the result of the Alfred Dreyfus case, Herzl realised that even in the civilised countries of France and Germany Jews were still viewed with suspicion. He wrote a book called *Der Judenstaat* – the Jewish State – as an expression of his political Zionism, his desire to see a modern Jewish state with a country, a flag and an identity. And of course there could be only one place for the realisation of this dream, Palestine, the historical land of Israel (even though Uganda was offered to him!).

Newspapers and other media sources today give the impression that Israel 'occupies' land once owned by people living in a 'Palestinian state'. But the evidence is to the contrary. For a start, the Arabs did not see themselves as 'Palestinians'. When the first congress of Muslim-Christian Associations met in Jerusalem in February 1919, the agreement was that 'we consider Palestine as part of Arab Syria'. The only people who considered themselves 'Palestinians' in the first half of the twentieth century were the Jewish inhabitants! Even the Jewish national newspaper was called *The Palestine Post* (now called *The Jerusalem Post*).

The other point concerns ownership of the land. Did Jewish immigrants seize it or was the land acquired legally? Land settled by these first immigrants in the 1880s was bought from the absentee Turkish landlords, who were eager for the extra cash. The land initially settled was the uncultivated empty land, swampy and cheap. Later on, they bought cultivated land, some of it at exorbitant prices. In his memoirs, King Abdullah of Jordan wrote *'The Arabs are as prodigal in selling their land as they are in useless wailing and weeping.'*[5] Up until 1948, with the formation of the State of Israel, no land was seized or acquired in any way other than through legal means.

In the twentieth century, Arabs as well as Jews were immigrating into Palestine, mainly from Egypt, Transjordan, Syria and Lebanon. Between 1922 and 1931, when the country was administered by the British, illegal Arab immigrants (i.e. extra to the agreed quotas) comprised almost 12 per cent of the Arab population. The Hope Simpson Report acknowledged in 1930 that there was an *'uncontrolled influx of illegal immigrants from Egypt, Transjordan and Syria'.*[6]

The key event of the early twentieth century for this region was the disintegration of the Ottoman empire as a result of them joining the losing side in the First World War. After the war, responsibility for the Land of Palestine fell to the British.

In 1917 Lord Balfour, the British Foreign Secretary, wrote the following to the Jewish community: *'His Majesty's Government view with favour the establishment in Palestine of a national home for the Jewish people and will use their best endeavours to facilitate the achievement of this object, it being clearly understood that nothing shall be done which may prejudice the civil and religious rights of existing and non-Jewish communities in Palestine, or the rights and political status enjoyed by Jews in any other country.'*[7] This was the Balfour Declaration and was made in part as thanks for the work done by Chaim Weizmann, a brilliant Jewish chemist, including his significant work for the British war effort.

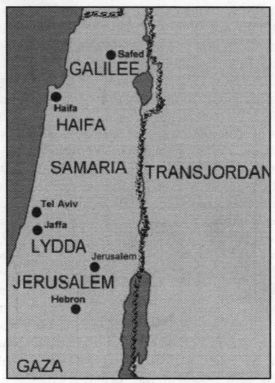

Fig. 8: **The British Mandate in Palestine (1920–1947)**

On December 11, 1917, General Edmund Allenby, a devout Christian, was handed the keys of Jerusalem, as

Britain's representative, by the defeated Turks. The rest of the country was conquered in the following year. At the San Remo conference in 1920, the League of Nations rubber-stamped this situation and Britain was officially given the Mandate for Palestine. Britain was now able to implement the Balfour Declaration and it would have done so had it not made similar promises to the Arabs. Jerusalem was declared an international enclave, neither Jewish nor Arab. So, with typical Britishness, a compromise was offered. The whole eastern part of the Mandate was given to a prominent Arab, Emir Abdullah, to thank him for helping them in their fight against the Turks. This became Transjordan, later to be renamed Jordan. Interestingly, the Emir wanted to call his land Palestine – if he had, perhaps he would have done us all a favour! So 80 per cent of the British Mandate was handed to the Arabs and Jewish immigration was completely banned in this area.

The rate of Arab immigration increased during the early 1930s, which was a period of prosperity in Palestine. The Syrian Governor of Hauran admitted in 1934 that 30,000–36,000 people from his district entered Palestine that year and settled there. In 1939 Winston Churchill said '*Far from being persecuted, the Arabs have crowded into the country and multiplied until their population has increased more than even all world Jewry could lift up (increase) the Jewish population.*'[8] This is an important (though much contested) point, because it dispels the myth that the Palestinian people have lived there for generations. When we talk about Palestinian refugees, displaced as a result of the formation of the State of Israel, consider how many of them would have been as recent to the land as the Jews themselves!

Jewish immigration continued and in 1929, there were about 150,000 Jews in the land, among 700,000

Arabs. But for Arab leaders this was unacceptable and there were many clashes, including a particularly nasty massacre of Jews praying at the Western Wall in Jerusalem and a similar one at Hebron. Incredibly, the British refused to allow Jews to defend themselves and 133 Jews were killed in subsequent riots. The British were becoming restless and in 1937 set up the Peel Commission, to suggest a further partitioning of the land. This would have given just the coastal plain, Galilee and Golan to the Jews, a corridor up to and surrounding Jerusalem to the British, and the rest, the largest area, to the Arabs. Surprisingly the Jews accepted this. Even more surprisingly, the Arabs rejected it, declaring that no Jewish state of any shape or form was acceptable. Arab revolts continued right up to the outbreak of the Second World War, when the Arab leaders opted for the side of the Nazis.

In 1939, at a conference in London, Britain suggested a new partition. This envisaged an Arab-dominated state: 75,000 Jews would be allowed in by 1944, and thereafter the Arabs could decide how many Jews to let in. Amazingly, the Arabs rejected this too! Yet the 75,000 quota was adhered to – a tragic state of affairs considering what was now beginning to happen in Europe. In early 1942, a ship with 769 Jewish refugees was refused permission to dock in Haifa and later sank. In 1947, the British refused entry to another ship, the *Exodus*, carrying 4,500 immigrants who were ultimately sent back to holding camps in Germany, of all places.

Britain was vilified by world opinion for these actions, particularly now that the horrors of the Holocaust had been uncovered. Losing patience with the terrorism of both the Arab and Jewish extremists, and preoccupied with holding together its ailing empire, Britain finally decided that enough was enough and handed the problem to the newly formed United Nations to sort out.

What was proposed was a partitioning of the land into three portions: an Arab state, a Jewish state and an international area based around Jerusalem. The Jewish state was to be a strange twisted area, lassoed at two points and destined to be the ugliest-looking bit of geography on the map. The Arab state fared little better, being the photographic inverse of the Jewish state except for a large hole in the middle, the international area. Only a committee could have come up with such a hotchpotch!

On November 29, 1947, the General Assembly of the United Nations met to see what to do about the situation. We'll see what happened there in the next chapter, but first, what did God think of all this?

It is difficult for us, with our imperfect mortal minds, to understand that God would still remember the Jews after so long. After all, thanks to the actions of the Christian establishment over the previous 13 centuries, their existence had been very precarious. As unlikely as it may have seemed, the fact remains that God was going to have His way despite the actions of the Church. He was going to honour His covenant with the descendants of Abraham. Let us remind ourselves what it involved. We read in Genesis 13:14–15 '*The LORD said to Abram after Lot had parted from him, "Lift up your eyes from where you are and look north and south, east and west. All the land that you see I will give to you and your offspring for ever."*' And now, after centuries of exile, they had returned to see the start of the fulfilment of this ancient promise.

Just as He had ensured the existence of Judah when Israel had been absorbed into the Gentile Assyrian world, He was not going to abandon His people now. He worked in the way He always works, for His Name's sake, as an expression of His holiness. He is a consistent, honourable God. If He makes a promise, He will make sure He keeps it, despite the actions of others, even those who claim to be His followers.

It is worth remembering here the words of Jeremiah the prophet, in Chapter 31, verses 35–37: *'This is what the* LORD *says, he who appoints the sun to shine by day, who decrees the moon and stars to shine by night, who stirs up the sea so that its waves roar – the* LORD *Almighty is his name: "Only if these decrees vanish from my sight," declares the Lord, "will the descendants of Israel ever cease to be a nation before me." This is what the* LORD *says: "Only if the heavens above can be measured and the foundations of the earth below be searched out will I reject all the descendants of Israel because of all they have done," declares the* LORD*.'*

How clear can you get! The sun, moon and stars would cease functioning before God would give up on His people, the Jews. Every inch of the heavens and the earth would be explored and measured before His people are cast away! So the Jews were kept intact not only through the hostile empires of Bible times – the Babylonians, Greeks and Romans – but also during the 13 centuries of 'State Christianity', surviving marginalizations, expulsions, massacres and pogroms at the hands of the followers of the *Jewish* Messiah! But survive they did, so much so that when we arrive at the year 1947, this nation without a land could not remain so any longer.

NOTES

[1] JC Ryle, *Are you ready for the end of time?* (Christian Focus Publications, 2001), pp. 105–124.

2   Sir John William Dawson, *Modern Science in Bible Lands* (New York, 1890), pp. 449–450.

3   Alphonse de Lamartine, *Recollections of the East* (London, 1845), vol 1, p. 268.

4   Mark Twain, *The Innocents Abroad* (London, 1881), pp 349–375.

5   The full quote from the memoirs of King Abdullah is: '*It is made quite clear to all, both by the map drawn up by the Simpson Commission and by another compiled by the Peel Commission, that the Arabs are as prodigal in selling their land as they are in useless wailing and weeping*' (taken from Hope-Simpson report http:// www. palestinefacts.org/pf_mandate_hope_simpson.php).

6   Quoted in article *From time immemorial* by CFI UK on http://www.cfi.org.uk/fromtime.htm.

7   The full text of the Balfour Declaration is on http://www.mfa.gov.il/mfa/go.asp?MFAH00pp0.

8   Martin Gilbert, *Winston S Churchill, the Prophet of Truth*, (Boston, 1977), vol 5, p. 1072.

Chapter 8

Israel

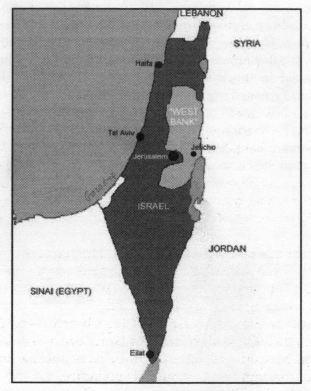

Fig. 9: **The United Nations Partition Plan 1947**

We now arrive at the point of focus, the one single issue at the heart of the major conflict of the modern world. It doesn't just divide Jew and Muslim or Palestinian and Israeli, but also Christian and Christian. It is the one issue where Mr Roots and Mr Shoots totally part company and Christian unity makes way for heated debate.

It is the question of the State of Israel.

Israel is a tiny country: the size of Wales, we're told. Its territory is less than 0.5 per cent of the landmass of its 21 hostile Arab and Muslim neighbours. It's so tiny that at one point it is barely nine miles across, yet the world screams at it for being expansionist! It's also the world's foremost political and religious hotspot, giving rise to more United Nations resolutions than all other nations put together! It's both hated and loved by more people than any other.

How can this be? How can such a tiny place generate such heat? These are understandable questions for someone who believes that the State of Israel is the product of historical processes, in much the same way as the other 300+ nations of the world. Such is also the reaction of Mr Shoots, whose theological views lead him to the conclusion that the Bible has absolutely no relevance to modern day Israel.

There can be no compromise. It is impossible to hold to Mr Shoot's theological position and admit that the survival of the Jewish people and the formation of Israel have anything at all to do with God.

The formula is set in stone. If the Church is the 'New Israel', then the Jews of the 'Old Israel' are a people discarded by God and, although they have somehow survived through 2,000 years of prejudice, hatred and extermination, it is just an accident. God is simply not interested in them; in fact, they seem to have survived *despite* His best efforts. They even survived the Holocaust, the biggest ever attempted genocide, which seemed, against all the odds, to lead to the first ever re-emergence of a nation some 3,000 years after it had last been a sovereign state.

A historical accident? Sure. Whatever. Just as an atheist sometimes has to show extraordinary faith in his belief in the absence of God, so Mr Shoots must exercise astounding faith in his position in the face of growing evidence to the contrary!

Be warned. If Mr Shoots is forced to make even the slightest concession of divine favour to the Jews, then his whole argument collapses and a rethink is needed. If the Jews possess just a crumb of divine favour then perhaps the 'Old Israel' is still a part of God's plan and what we are seeing with the Jewish people and Israel today is the survival of a remnant, a particularly typical feature of God's plans for mankind, whether through the prophets at the time of Elijah or, more pertinently, the *'remnant chosen by grace'* in Romans 11:5. Take time to read this chapter of Romans and meditate on verses 11 and 12, which speak of the Jewish people:

> *'Again I ask: Did they stumble so as to fall beyond recovery? Not at all! Rather, because of their transgression, salvation has come to the Gentiles to make Israel envious. But if their transgression means riches for the world, and their loss means riches for the Gentiles, how much greater riches will their fullness bring!'*

Mr Roots looks at the evidence around him and comes to a rather different conclusion. He believes that the Bible has every relevance to modern day Israel. He remembers the eternal covenant that God made with Abraham, promising their continuance as a nation, their blessings to mankind (through Jesus) and their inheritance of the land of Canaan. He sees the exile from the land as a necessary outworking of God's righteousness concerning the enjoyment of this inheritance, but he also sees the other side of the coin. He looks at the survival of the Jews and the formation of the State of Israel and he sees miracle after miracle.

Miracle One. The time: November 29, 1947. The place: the United Nations General Assembly. The occasion: voting to decide on the UN Partition Plan to create a Jewish State and an Arab State.

Fifty-seven nations voted. Naturally the Muslim countries – Egypt, Iran, Iraq, Lebanon, Pakistan, Saudi Arabia, Syria, Turkey, Yemen and Afghanistan – voted against the plan, not wanting any official declaration of a Jewish nation in their midst. Britain, to its shame in view of its century-old relationship with the Jews, abstained; its pride wounded by its failure in the area.

The biggest mystery concerned the attitude of the Soviet Union, which actually saw the Jewish Zionists, with their socialist leanings, as potential allies in the Middle East. So the USSR and its allies joined with Europe and most of the free world and voted for the partition plan. Without this unexpected support the United Nations partition plan would never have been accepted, as it needed a two-thirds majority to be carried through. But carried through it was, and the State of Israel was born into the international community.

Israel was once again a nation after centuries of exile, and the words of Isaiah 66:8 seemed to speak volumes: *'Who has ever heard of such a thing? Who has ever seen such things? Can a country be born in a day or a nation be brought forth in a moment? Yet no sooner is Zion in labour than she gives birth to her children.'*

But the birth was not an easy one. We fast-forward to May 14, 1948, the date of the declaration of the State of

Israel. A nation was born. Miracle two.

The odds were 200 to 1: seven Arab nations with a population of over 140 million against one fledgling Jewish nation with 650,000 people. The Arabs driven by hatred and pride, the Jews driven by the need for survival and the desire to put the Holocaust behind them. The Jews had no backing from any other country. The Arabs had, amongst other advantages, a British-sponsored army called the Arab Legion. Israel was fighting on four fronts: Transjordan to the east, Lebanon to the north, Iraq and Syria in the north-east and Egypt in the south. It was 1948 and this was Israel's War of Independence.

The Jews had little military equipment, especially arms and ammunition – at times two soldiers had to share a single rifle. During the war, they used weapons foraged and specially created, such as improvised armoured cars and Molotov cocktails. They also had a mixture of small arms left over from the Second World War, light artillery and machine guns, some anti-tank bazookas, and jeeps and half-tracks with mounted machine guns. The Arab armies, on the other hand, were heavily armed with the latest equipment from Britain.

But God hadn't brought His covenant people, the Jews, this far just to leave them in the lurch. The war lasted over eight months, punctuated by the occasional truce. The Israeli victory was such that only a quick intervention by British delegates in the UN saved the Arabs from a more disastrous defeat.

The war that was provoked by the Arabs to annihilate the new State of Israel not only brought a pride-thrashing defeat for them but rewarded the Israelis with over 40 per cent extra land over and above that promised to

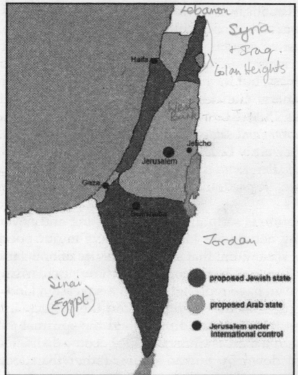

Fig. 10: **Israel after the War of Independence 1948**

them through the UN Partition Plan, including West Jerusalem! It was only thanks to the effectiveness of Sir John Glubb and his Arab Legion that the Israelis didn't take the whole of Jerusalem, including the Wailing Wall, the holiest site in Judaism.

Let us stop and think of what it was really all about. Do you really think that God wanted Jerusalem, His city, to be governed by an international committee? Do you really think that it was going to be easy for His people to be resettled in their ancient land? Of course not. It was going to be a real battle . . . literally!

The Israelis in 1948 were not, and are not now, as pure and spiritual as we'd like them to be. They were, and are, just as secular as the other nations around them, Britain included. They didn't deserve the land by virtue of holiness, but they inherited the land by virtue of their chosenness. God chose them to inherit the land in Genesis 15:18–21: *'On that day the Lord made a covenant with Abram and said, "To your descendants I give this land, from the river of Egypt to the great river, the Euphrates – the land of the Kenites, Kenizzites, Kadmonites, Hittites, Perizzites, Rephaites, Amorites, Canaanites, Girgashites and Jebusites."'*

Scripture is scripture; it is everlasting and never lies. We may not always like what it says in our politically correct society, but that's just a measure of how far away from God we have come and how secularism and humanism have replaced faith in a sovereign God. Let's not argue over the small print and the politics. Instead, let's get into the 'sacred print' and the spiritual picture. If we don't, then as Christians we become distracted and bogged down by human issues, rather than focus on divine ones.

The 1950s came. Jordan quietly annexed East Jerusalem, Judea and Samaria, calling it the West Bank. It never belonged to them; it was an illegal act. Only Britain and Pakistan recognised this move. Rather than calling the West Bank the 'occupied territories', we should remember that Jordan illegally occupied it first!

June 1967. God had rested on the seventh day, pleased with His creation. The Israelis, similarly, had much to be pleased about on their seventh day. Seven days earlier they had looked south and seen Egyptian tanks at the border with a blockade on Israeli shipping; to the north, Syria was bombarding Israeli villages from the Golan

Heights; to the east, Jordan and Iraq were gnashing their teeth, ready and waiting. War had not been officially declared, but you'd hardly believe it. The airwaves around Israel were full of boasting rhetoric, Arab nations vying with each other to be the first to 'liberate' Palestine. Nasser, the Egyptian leader, declared a *jihad*, a holy war, against the infidel Israel. They outnumbered Israel five to one in troops, three to one in tanks and nearly three to one in combat aircraft. Like schoolyard bullies, they postured and posed, growling and threatening destruction.

But the Israelis hadn't read the script. Orde Wingate, their British military mentor from the 1930s, would have been proud of them as they clinically unleashed one of the most decisive battle plans in military history.

On June 5, Israel attacked. It destroyed almost all of Egypt's air force, the largest in the Middle East, in three hours. Most of the planes hadn't even taken off. To all intents and purposes, the war was over. From then on confusion and fear reigned in the Arab forces. By the end of the week, Israel had captured Sinai and the Gaza Strip from Egypt, the West Bank and the rest of Jerusalem from Jordan, and the Golan Heights from Syria. Israel had increased its size by an incredible 300 per cent! Historian Cecil Roth later described the Six Day War as *'perhaps the most brilliant campaign in military history . . . The Israeli army had shown itself the best fighting force in the world.'*

The truly interesting fact concerns Jerusalem. Jerusalem wasn't included in the original UN Partition Plan agreed by the Jews, yet they took the western part of it as spoils of war in the War of Independence. Also, knowing that any battle for Jerusalem would be costly, the Israeli leadership tried to come to a compromise with Jordan over it during the Six Day War. But Jordan refused, having being confused by a false report that Egypt had destroyed the Israeli air force! So the Israelis took the whole of Jerusalem after the heaviest fighting of the war. It seems that Jerusalem was being coaxed into Jewish hands, by fate, by providence . . . or do we dare to say through a miracle of God?

Jerusalem in Jewish hands for the first time in 1,897 years. We are reminded of scripture. Luke 21:24 says *'They will fall by the sword and will be taken as prisoners to all the nations. Jerusalem will be trampled on by the Gentiles until the times of the Gentiles are fulfilled.'* Could this be the end of the times of the Gentiles, which began when the Romans destroyed Jerusalem in AD 70? Perhaps it was the beginning of the end of the times of the Gentiles. However you look at it, God was on the move.

We move on to 1973. So you want miracles? Then read on. Lance Lambert was a British Jew living in Israel at the time of this war, and he wrote of it in his book *Battle for Israel*:

> *'The Yom Kippur War should have been the annihilation of the State of Israel. People think of the 1967 Six Day War as a miracle, but it was nothing compared with the Yom Kippur War and in the years that lie ahead, when the whole truth comes out, we shall see that it was beyond all reason that Israel was not annihilated.'*[1]

He goes on to remark that at one point in the war only 90 battered Israeli tanks stood between the powerful Egyptian army and Tel Aviv and that both Egypt and Syria could have beaten Israel but were inexplicably prevented. Two episodes stand out. The first Egyptian tank division that crossed over the Suez Canal faced nothing to prevent it and the ones that followed behind from advancing into central Israel. Yet, inexplicably, it stopped. To the north of Israel the Syrians poured out of the Golan Heights, yet when they got within sight of the Israeli HQ and the Sea of Galilee they also mysteriously halted. What makes this story amazing is that the HQ was manned by just ten men and two tanks! Another story concerns an Israeli captain, a man without any religious beliefs. As he was fighting in the Golan, he looked up into the sky and saw a great grey hand pressing downwards as if it were holding something back. Lance Lambert's conclusion as to what was behind all these incredible events was that *'without the intervention of God, Israel would have been doomed'*.

The Yom Kippur War was an all-out attack on Israel by Egypt and Syria that took the country completely by surprise, not only because it happened on the holiest day in the Jewish calendar, but because for the first time the military and the defence establishment were totally unprepared. Unlike the Six Day War, this time Israel started out at a complete and utter disadvantage, with the element of surprise (helped by Soviet spy satellites) used against them. Yet, just as in the Six Day War and all other preceding conflicts, the outcome was totally in her favour.

At the start of the war, the world looked on, seemingly indifferent, preparing their best suits and mourning dresses for Israel's funeral. The United Nations held back for reasons that were all about politics, rather than intervening out of compassion for a fledgling country barely 25 years old.

But, wait, another miracle! Against all the odds, very soon Israel began to throw back the invading forces. She was near the gates of Damascus, the capital of Syria, and had surrounded the Egyptian third army in the south,

with Cairo in her sights. The United Nations was unprepared for this; it had already prepared the eulogy for the
death of a brave nation and was not expecting such ter-
ritorial aggression by the 'Zionist imperialists'. Incensed,
the UN immediately voted for a ceasefire before Israel
completely rewrote the map of the Middle East!

It was a great victory but a costly one for the Israelis –
$7 billion in money and 2,552 in lives, with over 3,000
wounded. Although the Arab losses were far greater in
numbers, proportionally to the size of the nations these
figures were a disaster for Israel. Very few families survived the war without having to mourn a personal loss.

Then there was the Gulf War. Operation Desert Storm
was a war fought between the oil-hungry West and a
fanatical dictator called Saddam Hussein who'd invaded
the nursery and pinched a few toys. Put it this way: if
Kuwait had produced fruit and not oil, no-one would
have given a fig! When political and economic interests
are concerned, moral issues can go out of the window!
Britain and other western nations had been profitably
arming Iraq since the Iraq/Iran conflict. All of a sudden,
the Iranians, who had recently been excommunicated,
were now our friends, along with the Syrians. Let's forget the Rushdie *fatwa*, we're all friends now, at least until
we get our toys back! If you think that's crazy and mixed
up, spare a thought for King Hussein of Jordan at this
time: on the one hand English-educated and a friend of
the British Royal Family, but on the other suddenly now
Saddam's biggest (and only) chum!

So where does Israel fit into all this? While the might
of the coalition forces was pounding the stuffing out of
Iraq's infrastructure and playing war games with com-
puters and thinking missiles, Iraq was lobbing 40 or so
Scud missiles at the 'Zionist Entity', hoping to lure Israel

into the conflict. A miracle of this indiscriminate and unprovoked attack was that only two people died as a direct result of the missile strikes, although others died of heart attacks brought on by stress. One interesting statistic that came out of this was that during this time, fewer Israelis died than would have been the case if life had been normal – there were fewer road accidents, for example.

After 40 days (a biblical number if there ever was one) of missile attacks on Israeli cities the war came to an end. And the biggest miracle of it all was that of all the days that the war could have ended, it had to end just before the most poignant day of all – Purim. Purim is the day of Jewish deliverance. A festival day of national rejoicing now had a special ring to it. The evil Haman, who tried to annihilate the Jews at the time of Queen Esther, now became the evil Saddam, who tried to knock out the Jews with Scud missiles. Saddam joined the long line of 'Hamans', symbols of anti-Semitic hate, and became a natural successor to Hitler, the previous 'Haman of this age'.

The intervening years from the Gulf War to the present day repeated more of the same. Israel with its back to the wall, increasingly isolated, Arab nations plotting its downfall and the Western powers formulating whatever selfish strategy they could to keep the oil pumping. Intifada, suicide bombing, propaganda, all these have been thrown at Israel with increasing ferocity. Modern times have become the most nerve-racking days in Israel's brief history, with each day adding a new twist. There must be barely a moment when an Israeli, whether under siege in a settlement, in the comparative safety of Tel Aviv or in the uncertain streets of Jerusalem, doesn't wonder 'What's going on, what's it all about?' To find an answer they must look upwards and inwards towards the God who, for the most part, they have deserted but who will never, according to His promises, desert them, the *'apple of His eye'*.

NOTES

[1] Lance Lambert, *Battle for Israel*.

Chapter 9

The 'Zionist Entity' and the West Bank

Fig. 11: **Israel after the Six Day War 1967**

When we think about all that has gone on so recently it is difficult not to get sucked into a fiery cauldron of emotion and political spin. Humanly speaking, it is hard to imagine a workable solution that would bring true peace to the region.

Let us review some of the human implications of this recent history.

In a nutshell, what happened was that the day after Israel became a country, it was invaded by Egypt, Transjordan, Syria, Lebanon and Iraq. Within a matter of weeks, against all odds, Israel was victorious, resulting in an expansion of territory and the displacement of hundreds of thousands of Arabs who had been living in Palestine.

As a result of these events, not one but two refugee situations were created. Just under 750,000 Arabs (UN estimate) lost their homes. These became the Palestinian refugees. They lost their homes for two main reasons. Some were driven out by the Jewish (Israeli) army, others fled after being told to do so by Arab army commanders, expecting an eventual victory (i.e. when the Jews would be driven out of the land), at which time people could return to their homes. Apart from extremists on either side, people generally accept these as the main reasons, though the proportions (i.e. what percentage were driven out or told to leave) would vary wildly, depending on your viewpoint.

The United Nations was strangely silent at the time, viewing the moving of populations and the creation of refugees as an unavoidable consequence of war. But it did have something to say about the Arab attitude, suggesting that they brought the whole thing on themselves. A report of the United Nations Palestine Commission just before hostilities stated '*Arab elements, both inside and*

*outside of Palestine, have exerted organized, intensive effort
toward defeating the purposes of the resolution of the General
Assembly. To this end, threats, acts of violence and infiltration
of organized, armed, uniformed Arab bands into Palestinian
territory have been employed ... The organized efforts of Arab
elements to prevent the partition of Palestine; the determined
efforts to Jews to ensure the establishment of the Jewish State
as envisaged by the resolution; and the fact that the Mandatory
Power, engaged in the liquidation of its administration and the
evacuation of its troops, has found it impossible fully to con-
tain the conflict, have led to virtual civil war in Palestine.'*[1] If
the Arabs had accepted the United Nations resolution
then, there would arguably have been no refugee crisis.

The Palestinian website http://www.palestinehisto-
ry.com/palst.htm concedes that *'about half probably left out
of fear and panic'*, which is a grudging concession to the
Jewish view. The quote continues, *'while the rest were forced
out to make room for Jewish immigrants from Europe and from
the Arab world'*. This leads us to examine the second
refugee situation, the lesser known and the largest one.

Until 1948, Jews had lived in most of the Arab Muslim
countries of the Middle East. In most cases, they had
been there over 1,000 years before Islam even existed.
From 1947, hundreds of Jews in Arab lands were killed
in government-condoned rioting, leaving thousands
injured and millions of dollars in Jewish property
destroyed. In 1948, Jews were forcibly ejected from Iraq,
Egypt, Libya, Syria, Lebanon, Yemen, Tunisia, Morocco
and Algeria, who confiscated property from the fleeing
Jews worth tens of billions in today's dollars. Of the
820,000 Jewish refugees created by this situation, 590,000
were absorbed by Israel.

All the facts presented so far are from an endlessly
contested history. People have argued about these facts

incessantly and have got nowhere in the process. So I'm now going to ask you to move on from the murkiness of endless debate and into the light of certainties.

The certainty is as clear-cut as they come. You can witness it with your own eyes. It is a fact that cannot be contested. Palestinian refugees *still* exist, in camps, on the West Bank, in Gaza and elsewhere. Why should this be?

The 820,000 Jewish refugees who were forcibly ejected from Arab countries where Jews had lived for thousands of years were all welcomed and integrated into Israel or the Jewish world elsewhere, where they became full citizens. There are *no* Jewish refugee camps.

The 750,000 Arab refugees who were displaced in 1948 were largely placed into squalid refugee camps by fellow Arabs who had just gone to war (and lost) on their behalf but were unwilling to pay for the consequences. Incredibly, over 50 years later, over a million of these poor people are still in these camps, despite billions of dollars of relief paid by rich Arab states, the United Nations, the EU and others. Where on earth has this money gone and why are they *still* in camps and not integrated into Arab society?

Palestinian Arabs are no doubt a peaceful, welcoming and gifted people, but they have been the greatest victims of the whole sorry affair, pawns in a wider struggle orchestrated by their powerful Arab brethren. For reasons known only to their political and religious masters they have lived for two or three generations within the bounds of these camps. Isn't a refugee camp meant to be a temporary home, as it has been for millions of refugees in other situations, until the people could be relocated to homes of their own? Not so here. Palestinians were never allowed to be 'ordinary' refugees. They have been kept in a form of forced captivity for a sinister purpose. A purpose that has succeeded in transforming a peace-loving, gentle people into terrorist pariahs and has provided an atmosphere where it is considered holy and noble to send your young men and women out as living weapons of destruction to blow up other young men and women. What must this do to their national psyche, when suicide is seen as a positive ideal? Let's be honest here and consider who is *really* responsible for this tragedy. It is not Israel. Can't they see who their real enemy is?

But they lost their homeland, you may say. This is true, though as I have suggested earlier, many would have been recent immigrants to the land rather than having lived there for generations, as suggested by the propaganda; and of course they were surrounded by oil-rich neighbours who shared their race, culture and religion. A homeland in Jordan, for example, would have been perfectly possible and logical. But let's look at it in a wider context. When I walk the streets and look around I see people of every hue and shade, I hear accents ranging from the Russian Urals to the Hindu Kush. These are not people who have been born in my country; these are people who have relocated here, many as refugees. There is nothing unique about Palestinians! Let's look at other recent refugee situations, as listed by the Encyclopaedia Britannica:

'The Russian Revolution of 1917 and the post-revolutionary civil war (1917–21) caused the exodus of 1,500,000 opponents of communism. Between 1915 and 1923 over 1,000,000 Armenians left Turkish Asia Minor, and several hundred thousand Spanish Loyalists fled to France in the wake of the 1936–39 Spanish Civil War. When the People's Republic of

China was established in 1949, more than 2,000,000 Chinese
fled to Taiwan and to the British crown colony of Hong Kong.
Between 1945 and 1961, the year that the communist regime
erected the Berlin Wall (opened 1989), over 3,700,000 refugees
from East Germany found asylum in West Germany . . . The
partition of the Indian subcontinent in 1947 resulted in the
exchange of 18,000,000 Hindus from Pakistan and Muslims
from India – the greatest population transfer in history. Some
8,000,000–10,000,000 persons were also temporarily made
refugees by the creation of Bangladesh in 1971 . . . During the
1980s and early '90s, the principal source of the world's
refugees was Afghanistan, where the Afghan War (1978–92)
caused more than 6,000,000 refugees to flee to the neighbour-
ing countries of Pakistan and Iran. Iran also provided asylum
for 1,400,000 Iraqi refugees who had been uprooted as a result
of the Persian Gulf War (1990–91). The break-up of
Yugoslavia, for example, displaced some 2,000,000 people by
mid-1992.'[2]

Then, of course, the Jews themselves over the last 3,000
years have been 'relocated' more times than you could
count.

And what of the West Bank, or the 'occupied West
Bank', as it is more often known? It is true that Israel
'occupies' the land since gaining it as a result of the victory in the Six Day War in 1967, but who did they take it
from? Well, actually, the West Bank itself was illegally
seized by Jordan after 1948. After doing so, they made it
an area forbidden to Jews! Who did Jordan take the West
Bank from? Before 1948, the West Bank was part of the
area administered by the British as part of the British
Mandate. It didn't belong to them, they were just care-
takers. Before that, the West Bank – called Judea and
Samaria by the Jews – was just the eastern part of

Palestine, occupied by whoever happened to live there, Jew or Arab. It was not land owned by any state, as Palestine was just a neglected province of the crumbling Ottoman empire. So, in reality, the West Bank has never legally belonged to any state in modern history. When Jewish settlers make their home there, they are doing so on land that has been legally bought, not seized from anyone else, whether a state or individuals.

In a sense, the political muddle is at centre stage because this is the time when God is taking a direct hand in the process, as foretold in His word.

His declaration is in Ezekiel, chapter 36. It's a long chapter, so I will just list the pertinent verses, though I urge you to read the full chapter yourself. I have also highlighted key parts.

Firstly, verses 1 to 12:

*'Son of man, prophesy to **the mountains of Israel** and say, "O mountains of Israel, hear the word of the Lord. This is what the Sovereign Lord says: The enemy said of you, 'Aha! The ancient heights have become our possession.'" Therefore prophesy and say, "This is what the Sovereign Lord says: Because they ravaged and hounded you from every side so that you became the possession of the rest of the nations and the object of people's malicious talk and slander, therefore, O mountains of Israel, hear the word of the Sovereign Lord: This is what the Sovereign Lord says to the mountains and hills, to the ravines and valleys, to the desolate ruins and the deserted towns that have been plundered and ridiculed by the rest of the nations around you — this is what the Sovereign Lord says: In my burning zeal I have spoken against the rest of the nations, and against Edom, for with glee and with malice in their hearts they made my land their own possession so that they might plunder its pasture-land." Therefore prophesy concerning the*

*land of Israel and say to the mountains and hills, to the ravines and valleys: "This is what the Sovereign Lord says: I speak in my jealous wrath because you have suffered the scorn of the nations. Therefore this is what the Sovereign Lord says: I swear with uplifted hand that the nations around you will also suffer scorn. But you, O mountains of Israel, will produce branches and fruit for my people Israel, **for they will soon come home**. I am concerned for you and will look on you with favour; you will be ploughed and sown, and I will multiply the number of people upon you, even the whole house of Israel. **The towns will be inhabited and the ruins rebuilt**. I will increase the number of men and animals upon you, and they will be fruitful and become numerous. **I will settle people on you as in the past** and will make you prosper more than before. Then you will know that I am the Lord. I will cause people, my people Israel, to walk upon you. **They will possess you, and you will be their inheritance**; you will never again deprive them of their children."'*

So where exactly are these 'mountains of Israel', where God's people, Israel, shall return to settle and rebuild? Look at any relief map of Israel and you'll see where the mountains are. They are not in the great centres of Jewish population – Tel Aviv, Haifa or even Jerusalem. They are in the central and eastern regions. Ironically, it is the very region offered to (and refused by) the Arabs by the United Nations in 1947: the land known as Judea and Samaria, also known as the West Bank.

The most controversial area in the Middle East also happens to be the very place earmarked by God as an area of Jewish immigration. What a coincidence!

The Jewish villages in this area are known as *yishuvim*. Israel calls them 'communities'. Outside Israel they are known as 'settlements in occupied territories', words tinged with the whiff of illegality. The world sees them as the chief obstacles to peace in the region. The settlers themselves, by and large observant Jews, would give just a single justification for their actions. They are obeying God's Word, from their reading of Ezekiel 36. Israel is a dangerous enough place to live in at the best of times, but the West Bank doubly so. Yet these Jewish settlers *choose* to live there, at whatever risk to themselves and their families. Most, including many in Israel proper, would call them deluded and provocative and wish they weren't there, but perhaps we should consider them in the same way as Christian missionaries in the jungles of Borneo. They are simply following the Word of God in their own way.

It is worth continuing to read from Ezekiel, chapter 36, to remind us about God's purposes in all this. We read in verses 22 and 23:

> 'Therefore say to the house of Israel, "This is what the Sovereign Lord says: It is not for your sake, O house of Israel, that I am going to do these things, but for the sake of my holy name, which you have profaned among the nations where you have gone. I will show the holiness of my great name, which has been profaned among the nations, the name you have profaned among them. Then the nations will know that I am the Lord, declares the Sovereign Lord, when I show myself holy through you before their eyes."'

Yes, it is all in God's plan. The West Bank is not the focus of the world's attention by accident or because the perceived injustices there deserve more newspaper coverage than the scores of other conflicts and age-old hatreds elsewhere in the world. God is intending this as a wake-up call. The settlers are not reading their scriptures selectively.

They can see that their return to the 'mountains of Israel' is not for their own wellbeing; they are doing it for the sake of the Lord's name. They should be commended for this, particularly as these verses are not exactly full of praise for the Jewish people. The world doesn't yet know our Lord, but the verses here tell us that, in a mysterious way that is yet to be unfolded, God is *going to use this situation to reveal himself.*

He gives a hint of this in the very next verses, 24 to 28:

> *'For I will take you out of the nations; I will gather you from all the countries and bring you back into your own land. I   will sprinkle clean water on you, and you will be clean; I will cleanse you from all your impurities and from all your idols. I will give you a new heart and put a new spirit in you; I will remove from you your heart of stone and give you a heart of flesh. And I will put my Spirit in you and move you to follow my decrees and be careful to keep my laws. You will live in the land I gave your forefathers; you will be my people, and I will be your God.'*

The Jewish people are not so intrinsically holy that their return to their ancestral land would create a shining light in the form of a society of perfect morality, impeccable ethics and an example for the world to emulate. This has been the mistake of many commentators who point at the State of Israel and say 'They're no better than any of us. How can they call themselves the "chosen people"?' This perception is so incorrect that it is downright laughable and shows a complete misunderstanding of the meaning of chosenness. God chose the Jews not because of any superior qualities they may possess. He chose them because He chose them, with the ultimate purpose of revealing Himself to mankind, as we read earlier in verses 22 and 23.

This is what JC Ryle knew a century earlier. The Jewish people are to return to the land in a *state of unbelief*. Only once they are in the land, at some unspecified time, will God's promise outlined in Ezekiel 36:24–28, quoted above, be fulfilled.

At the time of writing, this is still in the future, despite the growing number of Jews discovering Jesus their Messiah in Israel and elsewhere. But, when the time comes, God will act according to His words in verses 33 to 38:

> *'This is what the Sovereign Lord says: On the day I cleanse you from all your sins, I will resettle your towns, and the ruins will be rebuilt. The desolate land will be cultivated instead of lying desolate in the sight of all who pass through it. They will say, "This land that was laid waste has become like the garden of Eden; the cities that were lying in ruins, desolate and destroyed, are now fortified and inhabited." Then the nations around you that remain will know that I the Lord have rebuilt what was destroyed and have replanted what was desolate. I the Lord have spoken, and I will do it.' This is what the Sovereign Lord says: Once again I will yield to the plea of the house of Israel and do this for them: I will make their people as numerous as sheep, as numerous as the flocks for offerings at Jerusalem during her appointed feasts. So will the ruined cities be filled with flocks of people. Then they will know that I am the Lord.'*

Again, this is still to come, but make no mistake: when it does, the Jews and the whole world will know who is truly in charge.

But in the meantime, Israel has to live, as the 'Zionist Entity', in the face of its enemies' aim, clearly stated but now for reasons of political correctness not openly talked about, to 'drive the Jews into the sea'. This statement, made by the Egyptian leader Nasser in 1967, has never been publicly revoked and remains to every Israeli the stated purpose of Palestinian political pressure. The reason why it is not mentioned in Arab propaganda is simply that it wouldn't go down well in the corridors of power, newsprint and media channels in Europe and the USA.

Since September 11, 2001 the public has become more aware of the catalogue of hatred and invective directed towards Israel and the Jews from their Muslim Arab neighbours – but it is unnecessary for me to repeat this, as a daily reading of internet, satellite and terrestrial news sources would suffice. The key factor is blind hatred and, rather than reacting to it on an emotional level, we should seek to understand it in a wider context.

Why so much hate? Why have the Jews and every-thing associated with them attracted such negativity from those around them, whether Christian, Arab, Gentile, Muslim, and even other Jews? Is it because they are a *cursed* people and we are just seeing the outwork-ing of this, or is it because they are a *blessed* people, attracting resentment and anger? They can't be both, only one can be true . . . but which one is it?

NOTES

[1] The UN Palestine Commission report to the Security Council on February 16 1948.
[2] 'Refugees', *Encyclopaedia Britannica* CDROM.

Chapter 10

The Promised Land?

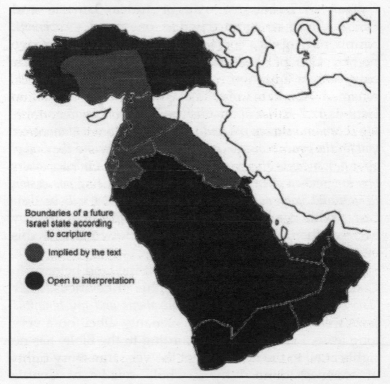

Boundaries of a future
Israel state according
to scripture

Implied by the text

Open to interpretation

Fig. 12: **Israel according to Genesis 15:18–21**

What's the connection between Kerala in India, Yorkshire in the UK and the USA in general? They have

143

all being variously described as 'God's Own Country'. The trouble is that these Indians, Yorkshiremen and Americans are all totally mistaken. There is only one country that God calls His own: Israel. The conflict over who owns the land is not a two-way fight between Jew and Arab; there are three 'corners' in this ring and there can only be one winner – God Himself.

The 4,000-year history of the Promised Land, from Canaan to Israel, by way of Judea/Samaria and Palestine, can be summarised in one word – *covenant*. Simply put, this is a contract or agreement between two parties. One of these parties was God and, for the covenant in question, the other party was Abram, renamed Abraham after the covenant was made, in Genesis 17:7–8: *'I will establish my covenant as an everlasting covenant between me and you and your descendants after you for the generations to come, to be your God and the God of your descendants after you. The whole land of Canaan, where you are now an alien, I will give as an everlasting possession to you and your descendants after you; and I will be their God.'* With regard to the land in question, history between then and now is simply the outworking of this everlasting, unconditional covenant.

The first point to consider is that the land belongs to God and God only. He confirms this in Leviticus 25:23: *'The land is mine and you are but aliens and my tenants.'* Jews were, and still are, God's tenants, albeit on a very long lease. Everyone else, according to the Bible, has no rights at all to the land, except the very transitory rights of conquest claimed by a whole swathe of Gentile invaders and occupiers, including Canaanites, Philistines, Greeks, Romans, Turks and Britons.

In an ideal world, Abraham and his descendants would have dug in their heels and continuously occupied the land as legal tenants from then to now. But this is not an ideal world and other factors came into play, not least the actions of these tenants. Their actions, whether idolatry, faithlessness or corruption, would never cause God to tear up the tenant's agreement, because the small print contained no conditions that the tenants should abide by. But their actions could result in the loss of blessings through expulsions from the land for varying periods.

God laid this out clearly through the writings of Moses in the Book of Deuteronomy, in the blessings of obedience and the curses of disobedience. He summarises the situation in Chapter 30, verses 19–20: *'This day I call heaven and earth as witnesses against you that I have set before you life and death, blessings and curses. Now choose life, so that you and your children may live and that you may love the Lord your God, listen to his voice and hold fast to him. For the Lord is your life, and he will give you many years in the land he swore to give to your fathers, Abraham, Isaac and Jacob.'*

All they had to do was choose life, which simply meant following the Lord and obeying His commands. Blessings for obedience are laid out in Chapter 28 – healthy children, good crops, defeat of their enemies, rain and prosperity. Yet *curses* are also laid out for disobedience – hunger, disease, destruction by their enemies and, ultimately, expulsion. God in His wisdom foresees all these things, knowing in advance that His people would turn against Him and reap the consequences. Having said that, He also looks ahead, in Chapter 30, to a regathering from exile. The words used are *'gather you again from the nations'* and *'bring you to the land that belonged to your fathers'* and hope is therefore offered to His people, with a reminder that He has never forgotten their tenancy of the land, even in their years of exile.

The first exile from the land was at the hands of the
Assyrians and the seeds were sown during the reign of
King Solomon. Hints of strife to come were first given to
David after his adultery with Bathsheba, but it was
Solomon who really messed things up. In 1 Kings 11:9 we
read *'The LORD became angry with Solomon because his heart
had turned away from the LORD, the God of Israel.'* Solomon,
despite all the blessings that God had given to him earlier in his reign, finally succumbed to the seductive whis-
pers of his hundreds of foreign wives and   concubines
and *'followed other gods'*. The penalty was significant. The
kingdom would be torn in two, Judah and Israel, and it
was going to happen in the following generation.

Things got worse for the northern kingdom of Israel in
that next generation. The ruler, Jeroboam, was even
more of an idolater than his predecessor. 1 Kings 14:15
outlines the punishment for his crime: *'He will uproot
Israel from this good land that he gave to their forefathers and
scatter them . . .'* The fate of the northern kingdom was
sealed and it disappeared from history in the eighth century BC.

The full thrust of the curses for disobedience therefore
came into play for the kingdom of Israel. You'd think it
would serve as a warning to Judah, the southern kingdom. Unfortunately it didn't. Judah sank into the same
sins and the only reason why it didn't suffer the same
fate is given in 2 Kings 8:19: *'Nevertheless, for the sake of his
servant David, the Lord was not willing to destroy Judah. He
had promised to maintain a lamp for David and his descendants for ever.'* So when the Babylonians arrived in the
sixth century BC and Judah was led into captivity for its
sins, the exile was only to be a temporary one.

A few decades later, the Jews were allowed back into
their land by the Persians and stayed there for another

600 years, despite suffering 'under the cosh' of Greeks and Romans for much of that time. They may have been in the land, but not always as a free people. They were not particularly reaping the blessings outlined in Deuteronomy, though their disobedience didn't warrant destruction or exile. But something was going to happen during the Roman occupation that would change this situation for the worse, even though ironically this event was intended as a blessing to end all blessings.

That event was the coming of Jesus the Messiah. Jesus came as the promised 'anointed one' of Israel, prophesied in the Hebrew scriptures. This was a momentous event. Jesus was the fulfilment of the Torah and the Prophets (Matthew 5:17) and the agent of the New Covenant prophesied in Jeremiah 31:31–33. Yet, as we read in John 1:11, *'He came to that which was his own, but his own did not receive him.'* The Jews as a nation rejected his claims and ultimately rejected him.

His mission during his lifetime was to the Jews. In Matthew 15:24 he says *'I was sent only to the lost sheep of Israel.'* Yet, with the exception of a few apostles and disciples, these 'lost sheep' rejected him and left it to the Romans to administer their brutal justice in the form of crucifixion outside the city walls of Jerusalem.

A few days earlier he had prophesied over those very walls *'Look, your house is left to you desolate. For I tell you, you will not see me again until you say, "Blessed is he who comes in the name of the Lord"'* (Matthew 23:38–39). He knew what was coming around 40 years later, when those walls would be breached by the Romans and the city destroyed. He was also stating the conditions for his return. The world was, and is, having to wait a long time for that particular event.

When the Romans came in AD 70 and sacked Jerusalem, there was to begin a period of Jewish exile, the Diaspora, which would last around 1,800 years. The Babylonian exile was just 70 years and was for the sin of idolatry, so what sin could have been committed this time to warrant an exile of such a magnitude?

The Jewish Christian teacher Arnold Fruchtenbaum has a view that may be uncomfortable for some. He refers to a key passage in Matthew. In Chapter 12, verses 30–32, we read '*He who is not with me is against me, and he who does not gather with me scatters. And so I tell you, every sin and blasphemy will be forgiven men, but the blasphemy against the Spirit will not be forgiven. Anyone who speaks a word against the Son of Man will be forgiven, but anyone who speaks against the Holy Spirit will not be forgiven, either in this age or in the age to come.*'

The context of this proclamation is Jesus' healing of a demon-possessed man and the Pharisees' assertion that this was only possible because Jesus himself was demon-possessed, rather than indwelled by the Holy Spirit. This was the 'blasphemy against the Spirit', or the unpardonable sin, a sin so awesomely bad that it cannot be forgiven.

According to Dr Fruchtenbaum, this is a national rather than a personal sin, being '*the national rejection by Israel of the Messiahship of Jesus while he was present on the grounds of him being demon-possessed*'. This, he adds, '*is the most important single event in the life of the Messiah with the exception of his death and resurrection, because it sets the stage for Jewish history for the next 1,800 years or so*'.[1]

In short, the Jewish nation (specifically the religious leaders) brought on themselves the 1,800-year Diaspora not just by rejecting Jesus as Messiah but also by attributing his miraculous works to the power of Satan.

Another view harks back to the proclamation of Bar Kochba as the Jewish messiah in AD 132, as mentioned earlier. This was a very public denial of the claims of Jesus and instigated the final split between Church and Synagogue.

However we justify this exile theologically, there's no doubt that the full weight of the curses of Deuteronomy 28 came into play.

Consider the following threatened punishments in the light of history:

- Being scattered among all the nations, from one end of the earth to the other (verse 64).
- Finding no peace anywhere, no place to call your own, being overwhelmed with anxiety, hopelessness and despair (verse 65).
- Your life always in danger, day and night filled with terror, living in constant fear of death (verse 66).
- Your heart pounding with fear at everything you see, every morning wishing for evening, every evening wishing for morning (verse 67).

It all sounds so horribly familiar when we consider the precarious history of the Jewish Diaspora, from the early rejections in the fifth century to the Holocaust of the twentieth century.

It is at this point that Mr Roots and Mr Shoots part company. For Mr Shoots, the Jews now leave the story as far as God is concerned. They are no longer the *true Israel* and so no longer belong to God. The trouble is that they never did go away, did they? For Mr Roots, the story continues.

If the latter verses of Chapter 28 of Deuteronomy refer to the Diaspora, then what of Chapter 30? As mentioned earlier, in this chapter God also speaks of a *regathering*, an end to the Diaspora. Ever since the middle of the nineteenth century, thanks to the enlightened efforts of evangelical Christians, particularly in Britain, Jewish people were beginning to be attracted to Jesus, their Messiah. At about the same time Britain was experiencing the Great Evangelical Awakening. Also, at the same time, Zionism was born and Jews were returning in numbers to their ancient land. Could this all be connected? Scripture seems to think so, as a reading of the opening verses testifies: *'When all these blessings and curses I have set before you come upon you and you take them to heart wherever the Lord your God disperses you among the nations, and when you and your children return to the Lord your God and obey him with all your heart and with all your soul according to everything I command you today . . .'* (Deuteronomy 30:12).

Were these conditions being met, even if in a small way? God seemed to think so for, as the verses continue '. . . then the LORD your God will restore your fortunes and have compassion on you and gather you again from all the nations where he scattered you.'* Scripture was clearly indicating an end of this exile. It continues: *'Even if you have been banished to the most distant land under the heavens, from there the LORD your God will gather you and bring you back. He will bring you to the land that belonged to your fathers, and you will take possession of it.'* Jews were returning from as far afield as China, Australia and Brazil, all of them 'most distant lands'.

Then came 1967 and the restoration of Jerusalem to Jewish hands. Was it a coincidence that, at that time, there was an explosion of Jewish people becoming believers in Jesus the Messiah, particularly in the USA? The momentum has continued ever since and we are now in a situation of having more Jewish believers in Jesus worldwide that at any time in history since the early days of the Church. Jewish people were becoming blessed the world over – returning to the land for some, returning to Jesus for others. Some were even doubly blessed, with both.

Of course, it has not been an easy journey. There are forces out there for whom these double blessings are a curse. World opinion, Islam and Arab nations are all in opposition, but it is Satan who is most grieved. He has very special reasons for wanting the destruction of the Jewish people and certainly for not wanting them in their land and embracing their Messiah. Anti-Semitism, wherever it might be found, was his invention and it had failed. Jews had survived, as God had always promised. And they were back in their land, according to God's covenant with Abraham.

When we look at the current unfolding crisis in the Middle East, we are mistaken if we see it just as another Bosnia or Northern Ireland or South Africa. It is not a local disagreement; it is a crisis of world proportions. It's not just a 'Jew and Arab' thing and 'why can't they learn to live together'? It's not an 'evil Zionist empire disregarding the rights of the Palestinians' thing. It's not even a 'heartless Arab terrorists killing innocent Israelis' thing.

It is a spiritual battle, not a physical battle. God is telling us that Israel (*including* the West Bank) is His land and the Jews are His legal tenants, and it is Satan saying otherwise and using all within his arsenal to fight with, whether it be false religion, materialism or nationalism. Above all, he uses confusion as his main tactic.

Don't you find it strange that the really important things are so *confusing*? The Book of Revelation is the

only Bible book that tells us that we're going to be
blessed by reading it (Revelation 1:3), yet it's the one we
find the most confusing, so we tend not to read it.

In the same way, the Middle East situation is a confusing one, so we tend to ignore it or be content to have
a superficial understanding, usually based on whatever
has been fed to us by the media.

It is every Christian's duty in these perilous times to
take the time to grasp the important issues, because one
day you may be taken to task over your opinion. You
owe it to your God, who has given you life in this world
and the next, to understand what's really going on in
Israel.

A grave danger is to be sidetracked by human issues.
Yes, the Palestinians have had a hard deal, though not
just at the hands of Israelis. Yes, they have suffered to an
extent under Israeli rule, just as they suffered in Jordan
and Lebanon. Prejudices are a fact of fallen humanity –
ask a black man in the USA or an aborigine in Australia.
These are issues of human rights and inequality. But all
these concerns pale into insignificance when divine
issues come into play.

One of the hardest concepts for us to accept is that of
election, how God makes His sovereign choices. God
chose the Jews to inherit the land and it's not up to us to
take issue with Him over this choice. Romans 9:15 says '*I
will have mercy on whom I have mercy, and I will have compassion on whom I have compassion.*' He makes His choices
and doesn't feel the need to explain them or justify them
to us.

God chose the Jews to provide us with the Bible and
the messianic line leading to Jesus. He chose them to suffer, for His own reasons – we don't see people arguing
with that fact. But He also chose them to inherit the land

of Israel, unconditionally and forever. We have to learn to accept that fact.

And then there is Jerusalem.

Zechariah 12 provides us with an intriguing and alarmingly accurate modern commentary.

Verse 2 proclaims '*I am going to make Jerusalem a cup that sends all the surrounding peoples reeling. Judah will be besieged as well as Jerusalem.*' This is happening now: we are living in those times predicted over 2,000 years ago. Recently the United Nations made a resolution about Jerusalem according to which '*the decision of Israel to impose its laws, jurisdiction, and administration on the Holy City of Jerusalem was illegal and, therefore, null and void*'.[2] Not a single nation supported Israel in this resolution, with 145 in favour of it and 5 abstentions. But be warned: where the will of the nations is in opposition to the Word of God, there can only be one winner.

Returning to the next verse in Zechariah 12, '*On that day, when all the nations of the earth are gathered against her, I will make Jerusalem an immovable rock for all the nations. All who try to move it will injure themselves.*'

The land of Israel belongs to God; it is *His* land. The city of Jerusalem also belongs to God; it is His city. In Psalm 132:13 we read '*For the Lord has chosen Zion (Jerusalem), he has desired it for his dwelling*'. Can you think of any other city, anywhere in the world, that could attract such attention?

Jerusalem is unique. Just over a century ago, it was a wasted, ruined city, yet now it is the focus of world attention. Any explanation other than the 'spiritual' one is folly. We are entering dangerous times, prophetic times. We must learn to read the 'signs of the times' because there is much deception around. Above all, we must hold on to God's Word regarding that parcel of land in the

Middle East that can rightly be called 'God's own country'. Don't listen to the world and its rantings and don't
get sucked into politics, it is just a distraction. Hold fast to
the truth and pray for the peace of Jerusalem. As for the
future, it is already being written as you read this.

NOTES

[1]   Arnold Fruchtenbaum, *The Life of the Messiah from a Jewish
       Perspective* (Anchor Recordings), tape series.
[2]   Report of 79th plenary meeting, December 14 1993, at
       http://www.un.org/documents/ga/res/48/a48r059.htm.

Epilogue

God has provided us with the Bible to guide us towards a godly life and to allow us to know His ways. We follow the words of scripture, are blessed by them, and often are spurred into action by them. In the case of the subject of this book, that action is especially significant because it concerns one's views on a whole people, the Jews, and a whole nation, Israel. The question of Israel is one of the true 'hot potatoes' in the world today, and so one must tread carefully.

In the case of Mr Shoots, 2,000 years of history have influenced his view. How he comes to his particular theological position is a typical 'chicken and egg' situation. Either he is convinced by his theological arguments first, with his particular view of history regarding Israel and the Jews following on from them, or vice versa. And it's the *vice versa* that is borne out by the dark side of Christian history over the past 2,000 years, borne out by the tragedies of the Crusades, the Inquisition, forced expulsions and, ultimately, the Holocaust.

Is a particular reading of scripture regarding the Jews a justification for the blind hatred that has been shown by those professing a religion of love and forgiveness, or did the hatred come first? People who subscribe to the theological arguments of Mr Shoots should be aware of its limitations and implications because the spiritualising of scripture has provided the theoretical justification for some of the most shameful episodes in Church history.

This is not to say that Mr Shoots is anti-Semitic, merely to say that 'Christian' anti-Semitism has often found a fertile ground in the views expressed by Mr Shoots.

If my words have offended you then I apologise, because I know that taking this theological view doesn't automatically mean you are anti-Semitic. The vast majority of you who hold this view are, I am sure, completely sincere in your beliefs and have arrived at your position with an open mind. All I would ask you to do is to persevere with my argument and then agree to disagree, amicably and in Christian brotherhood.

Arguments presented by Mr Shoots have been used by such church luminaries as John Chrysostom, Augustine, Tertullian, Origen, Irenaeus and Martin Luther, mentioned in the first chapter of this book.

It wasn't long before their theology and teachings gave way to practical action in the form of persecution, expulsion and extermination, solely on the basis of the arguments that the Jews had been *replaced* by the Church. Although in our day the Church has laid aside this physical action, the theology that inspired it is still with us. You must really consider what God's views would be on an interpretation of His scripture by leading Christian teachers throughout history that could inspire such shameful behaviour.

It is a sad fact that one of the most unifying concepts through Church history has not been theology or the teachings of Jesus, but negativity towards the Jewish people. That is putting it mildly!

And if you think I am being unnecessarily alarmist and extreme then I refer you to the cover story of *The Spectator* on February 16, 2002. It was entitled 'Christians who hate the Jews' and was written by Melanie Phillips, a Daily Mail journalist.[1] She was reporting on a meeting of Jews and prominent Christians brought together to discuss the churches' increasing hostility towards Israel. She wrote *'The real reason for the growing antipathy [to Israel], according to the Christians at that meeting, was the ancient hatred of Jews rooted deep in Christian theology and now on widespread display once again . . . The Jews at the meeting were incredulous and aghast. Surely the Christians were exaggerating. Surely the Churches' dislike of Israel was rooted instead in the settlements, the occupied territories and Prime Minister Ariel Sharon. But the Christians were adamant. The hostility to Israel within the Church is rooted in a dislike of the Jews'* (my emphasis).

The Christians at that meeting affirming this view were the editor of the main Church of England newspaper, the Archbishop of Wales (now the Archbishop of Canterbury), the Middle East representative of the Archbishop of Canterbury and the head of a Christian institute and relief organisation, who remarked *'What disturbs me at the moment is the very deeply rooted anti-Semitism latent in Britain and the West. I simply hadn't realised how deep within the English psyche is this fear of the power and influence of the Jews.'*

Anti-Semitism is alive and well and thriving in a church that has not heeded the errors of history. Martin Luther may have been the guiding light of the Reformation, but his anti-Semitism gave the green light for twentieth century German Lutherans to endorse the demonic views of Adolf Hitler, who even quoted from him in *Mein Kampf*!

Now ask yourself the following questions:

- Do you believe the Jewish people are eternally cursed as a result of their rejection of Jesus?
- Do you believe they have forfeited their right to be the 'chosen people'?
- Do you believe that Christians have supplanted the Jewish people as the only 'people of God'?

If you still truthfully believe in this final statement, ask yourself one fresh question:

- If God can reject his Old Testament people for their sins, why would a God of justice not reject his New Testament people for committing the very same sins and more? (Any reading of Church history will bear testimony to this.)

Now what I am *not* saying is that Jewish people as individuals have automatic entry to the blessings of eternal life. A Jew does not have personal salvation just because he was born a Jew. There is **only one way to salvation**, for Jew and Gentile, and that is through Jesus Christ. This book is not about individual Jews, it is about Jews as a nation, as a people, particularly in relation to the 'Land of Many Names'.

> *'This mystery is that through the gospel the Gentiles are heirs together with Israel, members together of one body, and sharers together in the promise in Christ Jesus'* (Ephesians 3:6).

Melanie Phillips, author of the article in *The Spectator*, received a lot of flak from Christians as a result of what she wrote. She subsequently wrote, on a website, *'Many mainstream Christians went into denial. I had spoken to exceptions on the fringe, they protested, and replacement theology no longer existed. But it is quite clear, not just from what I was told but from what I have read of very influential Christian texts, that a hatred of Israel is being underpinned by a theological analysis which implies, at root, that the Jews must be punished by the loss of their homeland for their refusal to believe in Christ.'*[2]

She was saddened and frightened by the re-emergence of an anti-Semitism that many thought dead and buried in the gas ovens of the Holocaust and, like many secular Jews, was amazed and horrified to find it still alive and well in the Church, of all places. Her conclusion is poignant, but a cutting indictment of the 'Christian Zionists' (our Mr Roots):

'In the depths of this moral darkness in which the Jews now find themselves besieged and almost alone and in which Israel's existence is threatened, the voices of the Christian Zionists are unwavering in their support and solace. Yet mainstream Christians denounce them. The Christian Zionists, they say, are no friends to the Jews since they would eventually have them all converted at the Second Coming. Well, if it comes to a choice between that and those Christians who would deny us our right to self-determination, make excuses for those who wish to kill us, peddle lies and write books inciting hatred against us, I think I know rather better where my friends are to be found.'

And what of the future? For Mr Roots, the future of our world is very much affected by the future of Israel and the Jewish people.

God's future for Israel? It's either an easy one to answer or a hard one, depending on how you look at it. The easy answer is that one day Jesus will return and all will be neat and wonderful (at least for those who believe in him). The hard bit is when we try to fill in the details between now and that glorious day.

So what do we know about the return of our Messiah? Jesus himself spoke of it in Matthew 24. He mentioned the signs that would precede that day, the deceptions and false prophets, the wars and rumours of wars, the famines and earthquakes, the persecutions, the falling away, the preaching of the Gospel to all nations. There has also been a hidden clock ticking away, visible but largely ignored. This clock is the Jewish people themselves and it's all to do with 'times and seasons'.

We start with what the apostle Paul calls a mystery. In Romans 11, he speaks about the future of the Jewish people. In verse 25 he says '*I do not want you to be ignorant of this mystery, brothers, so that you may not be conceited. Israel has experienced a hardening in part until the full number of the Gentiles has come in. And so all Israel will be saved . . .*'

There are three points to make here:

Firstly, it is a mystery and so we'll never really understand it, nor should we try, as our brains are simply incapable of the task. Some groups hate this idea, they feel that they should be able to explain everything and are unwilling to accept that there are some things in God's Word that are just for Him to understand. If God says something is a mystery, we should just accept it and work through the consequences. Let's face it, when Jesus was asked about the timing for the end of the world, he said '*No-one knows about that day or hour, not even the angels in heaven, nor the Son, but only the Father*' (Matthew 24:36), and that should be good enough for us.

The consequences here are that there has been a hardening in Israel. This is a sacrificial hardening, though Jews have largely been unaware of their sad role. Jews have been hardened in some way so as to allow Gentiles into the kingdom. Remember this is a mystery, so I don't have to explain it, but you'll do well to read the whole of Romans 11 and ask God to explain Himself to you. The hardening is also temporary and is due to end when the full number of the Gentiles has come in, when all Israel will be saved, whatever that means.

We would do well to look at the current world situation, with Jews flocking to the Gospel of Jesus the world over, as never before, or at least since the time of the Book of Acts, and consider the possibility that this hardening is finally coming to an end. This would also indicate that we are approaching the time when the full number of the Gentiles has come in. This ties in with one of Jesus' signs for his return, in Matthew 24:14: '*And this gospel of the kingdom will be preached in the whole world as a testimony to all nations, and then the end will come.*'

Luke 21:24 also speaks of the 'times of the Gentiles' and the idea that these will one day come to an end. This is part of the same 'end time' speech by Jesus. It reads '*Jerusalem will be trampled on by the Gentiles until the times of the Gentiles are fulfilled.*' Jerusalem has been in Jewish hands since 1967 and this is not a situation likely to change, despite the posturing and rantings of the nations of the world.

The Jews are not going to let go of Jerusalem now: it is their political and spiritual capital. It is also the most prophetically sensitive place on earth and the Lord, in His wisdom, spoke of the current situation over 2,000 years ago in Zechariah 12. He said '*I will make Jerusalem an immovable rock for all the nations. All who try to move it will injure themselves*' (verse 3). So be warned, United Nations: you're treading on dangerous, to say nothing of hallowed, ground.

Jerusalem is the place where the lonely and isolated nation of Israel will come into stubborn conflict with the rest of the world. But again, be warned, nations of the world, because we can carry on reading in this same oracle in Zechariah, *'I will keep a watchful eye over the house of Judah, but I will blind all the horses of the nations'* (verse 4). We can expect God to protect His people, which doesn't bode too well for Israel's enemies, whoever they may be.

We now return to Jesus' speech on the signs of the end of the age or, to be precise, his last words to the religious and political leaders of Israel, just before he explains himself to his disciples. He spoke prophetic words in Matthew 23:37–39: *'O Jerusalem, Jerusalem, you who kill the prophets and stone those sent to you, how often I have longed to gather your children together, as a hen gathers her chicks under her wings, but you were not willing. Look, your house is left to you desolate. For I tell you, you will not see me again until you say, "Blessed is he who comes in the name of the Lord."'*

This echoes part of Psalm 118, a messianic psalm looking ahead to the Messiah. It is also a theme in Hosea: *'Then I will go back to my place until they admit their guilt. And they will seek my face; in their misery they will earnestly seek me'* (Hosea 5:15).

Taking an informed glance into the future, I would suggest that there is going to be a time, perhaps soon, when the political and religious leaders of the nation of Israel will have to acknowledge the God of Israel. They will have to swallow their pride, despite having the third largest army in the world and the brains and ingenuity to deploy this army in unexpected ways. They are going to have to realise that it was the God of Israel who sustained them through the perilous times of the twentieth and twenty-first centuries in the land, just as He had sustained them in the preceding 18 centuries outside the land. I'm afraid the journey to this realisation from where they are now is not going to be an easy one and we can only pray that it will be short. Pride is surely the deadliest sin of all and needs to be dealt with convincingly, before God can really work with His people.

God needs His Jewish people to call on Him, to cry out to Him, before He can really act. In fact, the whole world needs this to happen, as we can see if we return to Matthew 23:39: *'For I tell you, you will not see me again until you say, "Blessed is he who comes in the name of the Lord."'*

Jesus here is giving a key condition for his return. He will only return when they, the leaders of the Jewish nation, welcome his return. Jesus will only return when the current leaders of Israel, from the Chief Rabbi to the Prime Minister, finally realise that he is the one that he had said he was, the promised Messiah. And for that to happen we are looking at a real miracle, because before they can ask him to return, they have to believe in him. They have to believe that he came, 2,000 years earlier, as their Messiah. And to do that they will have to admit that their predecessors made a grave, tragic, heart-wrenching mistake, a mistake that led to 1,800 years of sheer misery. And to do that their pride has to be broken, so that God can do a mighty work in the heart of the nation of Israel.

Incidentally, Mr Shoots, if the Jews are no longer God's people, what could Matthew 23:39 be speaking about? As there are no subsequent biblical records of Jesus appearing to the Jewish people en masse, this verse can only be referring to some future time when Jews will again see their Messiah.

It may seem unlikely, but scripture says it's going to happen. Returning to Zechariah Chapter 12, we see this theme repeated: '*Then the leaders of Judah will say in their hearts, "the people of Jerusalem are strong, because the* LORD *Almighty is their God"*' (verse 5). This is at the time when the nations of the world come against Jerusalem, and the warning that I gave earlier concerning these nations must be repeated, because verse 9 pronounces a dire warning: '*On that day I will set out to destroy all the nations that attack Jerusalem.*'

What an awesome day that will be. God will show His power, stronger than any Cruise or Scud missile, and the whole world is going to realise what a terrible mistake it has made in turning its back on the one true God. The Jewish people will particularly be affected as the truth finally dawns on them. Their reaction to this knowledge will be significant. We read in the very next verse, verse 10: '*And I will pour out on the house of David and the inhabitants of Jerusalem a spirit of grace and supplication. They will look on me, the one they have pierced, and they will mourn for him as one mourns for an only child and grieve bitterly for him as one grieves for a first-born son.*'

The awful realisation of the identity of Jesus their Messiah, the '*one they had pierced*', will initiate a national repentance the like of which the world has never seen before. The next three verses bear testimony to this, speaking of every clan in the land weeping and mourning. Then, perhaps led by their religious leaders, Orthodox and Messianic believers together (though, of course, all will now be 'Messianic'), they will sing the messianic Psalm, Psalm 118, as Matthew 23:39 tells us, and the Lord Jesus will return.

And where will he return? Certainly not in the world capitals of London, Paris or Washington. A clue is given in Acts, Chapter 1. The scene is the Mount of Olives, overlooking Jerusalem on the east side. Jesus is with his disciples for one last time, when suddenly a cloud hides him from their sight and he is taken back into heaven. His last words to them are in verse 11: *'This same Jesus, who has been taken from you into heaven, will come back in the same way you have seen him go into heaven.'*

He is going to return in the same way that he went – down from heaven, on the Mount of Olives. If you complain that I'm reading too much into the text, then head to Zechariah, Chapter 14. We read another account of that final battle over Jerusalem. More depressing details are given but again we are told that it is God Himself, or specifically the Messiah, who will fight against these armies of the nations. In fact, it's the first thing he does when he returns. Verse 4 tells us *'On that day his feet will stand on the Mount of Olives, east of Jerusalem, and the Mount of Olives will be split in two from east to west, forming a great valley, with half of the mountain moving north and half moving south.'*

It is going to be a truly awesome sight and the very geography of the region is going to be altered as a result. The Mount of Olives will be split in two and we read of a great river forming, flowing from east to west.

Jesus will return as Messiah King. No longer the suffering servant, the son of Joseph of his first coming. This time he will come to reign among his people, as the Son of David. He will come to live out those Old Testament scriptures that were not fulfilled by his first coming. For example, Isaiah 2:3–4: *'Many peoples will come and say, "Come, let us go up to the mountain of the Lord, to the house of the God of Jacob. He will teach us his ways, so that we may walk in his paths." The law will go out from Zion, the word of the Lord from Jerusalem. He will judge between the nations and will settle disputes for many peoples. They will beat their swords into ploughshares and their spears into pruning hooks.*

Nation will not take up sword against nation, nor will they train for war any more.'

Did any of this happen in his first coming? Of course not! As Christians, we defend ourselves against our scoffers, particularly Jewish ones, who quote from the above verses and say 'Your Jesus didn't bring in this great messianic age, so obviously he failed!' We answer this by talking of a *Second* Coming, when he will return as King to judge the world. Yet when some of us say as Christians, from a clear reading of scripture, that the Jews are returning to the land a *second* time, other Christians become scoffers. It's strange, isn't it? Anyway, back to the narrative . . .

Among the many other similar prophecies, we read in Daniel 7:13–14 *'In my vision at night I looked, and there before me was one like a son of man, coming with the clouds of heaven. He approached the Ancient of Days and was led into his presence. He was given authority, glory and sovereign power; all peoples, nations and men of every language worshipped him. His dominion is an everlasting dominion that will not pass away, and his kingdom is one that will never be destroyed.'* This is a picture of the Messiah that was not fully fulfilled when Jesus came 2,000 years ago.

If we continue with our look at Zechariah 14, we can fill in some of the details. In verse 9, we read that Jesus will now be king over all of the earth, a physical ruling king. And where will he rule from? Verse 16 onwards tells us. *'Then the survivors from all the nations that have attacked Jerusalem will go up year after year to worship the King, the Lord Almighty, and to celebrate the Feast of Tabernacles. If any of the peoples of the earth do not go up to Jerusalem to worship the King, the LORD Almighty, they will have no rain.'*

One day, the Lord Jesus is going to rule from Jerusalem, his city. This is the importance of Jerusalem, of Israel. This is also the importance of the Jewish people today living in the land promised to Abraham 4,000 years ago. Without Jews in the land, in Israel, the Word of God in Zechariah and in many other places just couldn't come to pass. The Bible would become a lie, which God would never allow to happen. When God was making that sacred covenant with Abraham, He knew that despite everything that was to happen, despite the pain and difficulties that He was to share with His people, history would come to pass as He had planned.

This is a good place for us to examine ourselves and consider the questions posed in this book. The fact remains that either:

- God has utterly rejected the Jews because of their sins and has abandoned them, demoting them from 'favoured nation' state to being just one people among many, *or*
- In exiling the Jews from the land, God was punishing His covenant people, but nevertheless He was holding up the promise of restitution to the land in the future.

They can't both be true!

One thing comes to mind, though, and this concerns the very character of God Himself.

If God had rejected the Jews after their rejection of Jesus, He would have been well aware of the consequences that would follow. He would have known that the Gentile Church would take on the role of proxy accuser and executioner, following the example of God's treatment of His other 'rejected' people, the Canaanites, who were 'ethically cleansed' by divine appointment, resulting in 1,900 years of anti-Semitism. In effect, if you'll excuse my directness, He was an *accessory before the fact* in this major crime, in committing an action that the Church felt empowered to follow through to its sad conclusion! Or perhaps I'm being a little too strong here and allowing my emotions to rule.

On the other hand, if all God was doing was punishing His chosen people, then the Church has been acting in direct opposition to His commands, heaping curse upon curse onto itself in the process. I think you will agree that any objective reading of Church history will bear evidence to the fact that it has hardly been a continuous catalogue of blessings.

In Chapter 8, I issued a warning to Mr Shoots. I suggested that if he is forced to make even the slightest concession of divine favour to the Jews, then his whole theological system collapses. If the Jews possess just a crumb of divine favour then perhaps the 'Old Israel' is still a part of God's plan and what we are seeing with the Jewish people and Israel today is the survival of a *remnant*, a particularly typical feature of God's plans for mankind.

So one last challenge to Mr Shoots. Please meditate on these historical facts before you lay the matter to rest:

- The continued existence of the Jewish people – in contrast to the disappearance of every other ancient people – after 2,000 years of severe persecution.
- The continued existence of Jewish culture – despite concerted efforts at assimilation into Gentile culture – after 2,000 years of severe persecution.
- Despite constituting 0.25 per cent of the world's population, since the twentieth century around 25 per cent of scientists have been Jewish.
- In 1978, over 50 per cent of Nobel Prize winners were Jewish.

- The three main intellectual architects of the twentieth century were Jewish – Karl Marx, Sigmund Freud and Albert Einstein (who was also declared 'Man of the twentieth century' by *Time* magazine December 31, 1999).
- The re-emergence of Hebrew, a dead language, as the spoken language of Israelis. (Do Italians speak Latin?)
- The formation of the State of Israel in 1947 by majority vote despite the fact that the majority of UN members were by inclination against the idea.
- The survival of Israel after the 1948 War of Independence with more land than was actually agreed in the UN Partition Plan.
- Jerusalem returning to Jewish hands in the 1967 Six Day War, virtually by accident!
- The cessation of Iraqi Scud missile attacks on the eve of Purim, the great festival of deliverance.
- The continued existence of the State of Israel despite its being surrounded by 21 hostile Nearly a million Jews being allowed to emigrate out of Russia.
- Israel has the highest number of scientists per capita of population in the world.

And finally, we return to JC Ryle, our nineteenth-century English Bishop. If you cast your mind back to Chapter 7, you'll remember that he wrote a sermon entitled *Scattered Israel to be Gathered*.

He made four points, the first three of which were 'Who is Israel', 'The present condition of Israel' and 'The future prospects of Israel'. His fourth and final point was 'The duty which the Gentile churches owe to Israel'.

He urges them to pray for and work towards the *spiritual conversion of Israel*. Then he commands them to *take stumbling blocks out of the way* of Israel. He teaches them not to follow the way of their forbears, by doing nothing to disgust Jewish people with Christianity or hinder their conversion. Also, he reminds them of the special blessings which God has promised to all who care for Israel. Everyone wants to be blessed, don't they? He quotes Psalm 122:6, concerning Jerusalem: *'They shall prosper that love thee'* and Numbers 24:9, concerning Israel: *'Blessed is he that blesseth thee and cursed is he that curseth thee'*. We would do well to meditate on these words.

I am very wary of debates, whether on TV or radio or in a packed hall. This is because, like many, I am easy prey for a silver tongue or an argument put forward with eloquence, authority and skill. On some issues, my views are so influenced by whichever articulate person I heard or read last that I can change my mind a dozen times a day. This is both laziness on my part and an acknowledgement that others are so much better informed than I that I'm happy for them to do my thinking for me. Now the arguments in this book may or may not be convincing to you. You could read books that promote the opposite viewpoint and perhaps be equally convinced. As I've said many times, the issue of Israel is too important for us to waste our time in endless debates rather than positive action, which is why I have laboured the point in this book.

I propose that we now move our attention away from these endless debates and, if you are still unconvinced by my arguments or if you are the type of person who needs more than words to convince you, then read on. Let us instead look at the evidences, the historical facts.

The evidences for the new life provided for those who
have embraced the Christian Gospel are plain to see – it
is in the new attitudes and actions inspired by their new
birth. Equally we can look at evidences for biblical teachings concerning the Jewish people and look again at the
two hypotheses that I stated earlier.

If, according to Mr Shoots, God has utterly rejected the
Jews because of their sins and has abandoned them,
demoting them from 'favoured nation' state to being just
one people among many, *where is the evidence?*

If, according to Mr Roots, the Jews were exiled from
the land as punishment from God, who still held up the
promise of restitution to the land in the future, *where is
the evidence?*

The fact is that Jews have survived 2,000 years of
extreme prejudice, returning to their ancestral land, a
return accompanied by incontestable miracles. Does this
point to a people cursed and abandoned by God, or a
people returning, for whatever reason, into God's
favour? If you are still unconvinced, just spare a thought
for the most ardent enemies of the state of Israel – militant Islam and humanism (man-centred philosophy).
Now spare a thought for the most ardent enemies of biblical Christianity in today's world. I would suggest the
same two – militant Islam and secular humanism. Is this
coincidental or significant? Where do you now think
God is in our debate over Israel, and which of our two
hypotheses do you think these facts provide evidence
for? I'll leave you to answer that question.

There is a massive deception in the world today that
has even infiltrated much of the Church. It goes like this:
If those stubborn and wicked Israelis give the stolen land
back to the Palestinians, all other conflicts will also go
away. Apparently the Muslim world would be so

placated that such people as Bin Laden and Saddam Hussein would just lay down their arms and the world would be a friendlier, happier place. Israel has become the scapegoat of the world, a role quite familiar to its Jewish inhabitants. In the Gulf War they were at the receiving end of Scud missiles, the World Trade Centre outrage was blamed on them by the Arab world, and the highly anti-Semitic *Protocols of the Elders of Zion* is a best seller among Egyptians and others. The West has bought into this idea, too, though it has often remained unspoken. When it is spoken, the words used are 'If you take away the cause of the Middle East conflict then the Muslims would stop hating us', meaning, 'Why doesn't Israel get its act together?' A demonstration in London in 2002 against a war against Iraq had as many slogans, displayed or chanted, concerning the Israel/Palestinian situation as there were concerning Iraq. If Tokyo was hit by an earthquake, I wonder how long it would be before the Jews were blamed?!

We are nearly at the end of our story. This is as good a place as any to provide a short summary of the position held by Mr Roots, a collection of his best arguments to provide you, at the very least, with food for thought after you put this book down. So here are his Top Ten arguments (in no particular order):

- Mr Roots interprets the Bible using principles followed by the earliest Christians, the Protestant Reformers and Jesus himself, and that is to give priority to the plain literal reading of scripture.
- Mr Roots stresses God's faithfulness in not breaking His unconditional covenant with the Jews. If He could, then why couldn't He do the same with His new covenant with Christians?

- Mr Roots doesn't need to re-interpret Old Testament scriptures in the light of the New Testament, a practice that leads to confusion, uncertainty and the need to rely on the teachings of theologians (who don't always agree with each other anyway).
- Mr Roots doesn't have to avoid the clear teaching of Romans 9–11.
- Mr Roots sees the Old Testament and the New Testament as a continuous whole rather than the New diminishing the importance of the Old Testament.
- Mr Roots takes a clear, sensible view of biblical prophecy, with literal rather than vague symbolic fulfilments. He is also able to view current world events through biblical eyes.
- Mr Roots doesn't have to ignore the clear teaching in the Psalms and Prophets of God's continuous love for the Jewish people, e.g. Jeremiah 31:37, *'This is what the Lord says: "Only if the heavens above can be measured and the foundations of the earth below be searched out will I reject all the descendants of Israel because of all they have done," declares the Lord.'*
- Mr Roots offers God's mercy and forgiveness to the Jewish people rather than providing the theological foundation for extreme hatred and persecution.
- Mr Roots offers reasonable explanations for the continuous existence of the Jewish people, the miraculous formation of Israel and the undeniably remarkable contributions of Jewish people to society.
- Mr Roots considers it more than a coincidence that God and Israel share the same common foes in the world today.

The current battle over the Holy Land is an important *spiritual* one. A battle is going to be fought over Jerusalem – and don't be fooled into believing that this is a local event, just an Arab-Israeli dispute. It is the God of Israel against all who oppose Him. It is no less than the climax of history, as unbelievable as it seems. We are indeed living in incredible times. Please pray for the peace of Jerusalem and the salvation of the Jews, and the Lord will surely bless you.

> *'God is spirit, and his worshippers must worship in spirit and in truth'* (John 4:24).

As Christians, we recognise that the whole point of our existence is to worship the Lord in spirit and truth; anything less just will not do. If your conscience is clear and you are being true to the promptings of the Spirit within you and true to the evidence of the written Word of God, then you are truly blessed.

Blessings to you all.

NOTES

1   Melanie Phillips, *Christians who hate the Jews*. The full article can be seen on http://www.spectator.co.uk. Do an author search on 'Phillips'.
2   Online Seminar at the Centre for Jewish-Christian Relations, *Replacement Theology*: presentation by Melanie Phillips. Found at: http://www.cjcr.cam.ac.uk/tfstuff/phillips.html

Recommended Reading

Bennett, Ramon, *When Day and Night Cease*, Arm of Salvation, 1992

Cohn-Sherbok, Dan, *The Crucified Jew*, HarperCollins, 1992

Dimont, Max I, *Jews, God and History*, Penguin, 1994

Fruchtenbaum, Arnold, *Jesus was a Jew*, Ariel Ministries, 1981

Katz, Samuel, *Battleground: Fact and Fantasy in Palestine*, Bantam, 1977

Richards, Rob, *Has God finished with Israel?* Authentic Lifestyle, 2000

Wilson, Marvin R, *Our Father Abraham*, Eerdmans, 1989

Recommended Reading